PERSIAN
VOCABULARY

ENGLISH-PERSIAN

The most useful words
To expand your lexicon and sharpen
your language skills

7000 words

Persian vocabulary for English speakers - 7000 words

By Andrey Taranov

T&P Books vocabularies are intended for helping you learn, memorize and review foreign words. The dictionary is divided into themes, covering all major spheres of everyday activities, business, science, culture, etc.

The process of learning words using T&P Books' theme-based dictionaries gives you the following advantages:

- Correctly grouped source information predetermines success at subsequent stages of word memorization
- Availability of words derived from the same root allowing memorization of word units (rather than separate words)
- Small units of words facilitate the process of establishing associative links needed for consolidation of vocabulary
- Level of language knowledge can be estimated by the number of learned words

T&P Books Publishing
www.tpbooks.com

ISBN: 978-1-78716-702-5

This book is also available in E-book formats.
Please visit www.tpbooks.com or the major online bookstores.

PERSIAN VOCABULARY
for English speakers

T&P Books vocabularies are intended to help you learn, memorize, and review foreign words. The vocabulary contains over 7000 commonly used words arranged thematically.

- Vocabulary contains the most commonly used words
- Recommended as an addition to any language course
- Meets the needs of beginners and advanced learners of foreign languages
- Convenient for daily use, revision sessions, and self-testing activities
- Allows you to assess your vocabulary

Special features of the vocabulary

- Words are organized according to their meaning, not alphabetically
- Words are presented in three columns to facilitate the reviewing and self-testing processes
- Words in groups are divided into small blocks to facilitate the learning process
- The vocabulary offers a convenient and simple transcription of each foreign word

The vocabulary has 198 topics including:

Basic Concepts, Numbers, Colors, Months, Seasons, Units of Measurement, Clothing & Accessories, Food & Nutrition, Restaurant, Family Members, Relatives, Character, Feelings, Emotions Diseases, City, Town, Sightseeing, Shopping, Money, House, Home, Office, Working in the Office, Import & Export, Marketing, Job Search, Sports, Education, Computer, Internet, Tools, Nature, Countries, Nationalities and more ...

T&P BOOKS' THEME-BASED DICTIONARIES

The Correct System for Memorizing Foreign Words

Acquiring vocabulary is one of the most important elements of learning a foreign language, because words allow us to express our thoughts, ask questions, and provide answers. An inadequate vocabulary can impede communication with a foreigner and make it difficult to understand a book or movie well.

The pace of activity in all spheres of modern life, including the learning of modern languages, has increased. Today, we need to memorize large amounts of information (grammar rules, foreign words, etc.) within a short period. However, this does not need to be difficult. All you need to do is to choose the right training materials, learn a few special techniques, and develop your individual training system.

Having a system is critical to the process of language learning. Many people fail to succeed in this regard; they cannot master a foreign language because they fail to follow a system comprised of selecting materials, organizing lessons, arranging new words to be learned, and so on. The lack of a system causes confusion and eventually, lowers self-confidence.

T&P Books' theme-based dictionaries can be included in the list of elements needed for creating an effective system for learning foreign words. These dictionaries were specially developed for learning purposes and are meant to help students effectively memorize words and expand their vocabulary.

Generally speaking, the process of learning words consists of three main elements:

- Reception (creation or acquisition) of a training material, such as a word list
- Work aimed at memorizing new words
- Work aimed at reviewing the learned words, such as self-testing

All three elements are equally important since they determine the quality of work and the final result. All three processes require certain skills and a well-thought-out approach.

New words are often encountered quite randomly when learning a foreign language and it may be difficult to include them all in a unified list. As a result, these words remain written on scraps of paper, in book margins, textbooks, and so on. In order to systematize such words, we have to create and continually update a "book of new words." A paper notebook, a netbook, or a tablet PC can be used for these purposes.

This "book of new words" will be your personal, unique list of words. However, it will only contain the words that you came across during the learning process. For example, you might have written down the words "Sunday," "Tuesday," and "Friday." However, there are additional words for days of the week, for example, "Saturday," that are missing, and your list of words would be incomplete. Using a theme dictionary, in addition to the "book of new words," is a reasonable solution to this problem.

The theme-based dictionary may serve as the basis for expanding your vocabulary.

It will be your big "book of new words" containing the most frequently used words of a foreign language already included. There are quite a few theme-based dictionaries available, and you should ensure that you make the right choice in order to get the maximum benefit from your purchase.

Therefore, we suggest using theme-based dictionaries from T&P Books Publishing as an aid to learning foreign words. Our books are specially developed for effective use in the sphere of vocabulary systematization, expansion and review.

Theme-based dictionaries are not a magical solution to learning new words. However, they can serve as your main database to aid foreign-language acquisition. Apart from theme dictionaries, you can have copybooks for writing down new words, flash cards, glossaries for various texts, as well as other resources; however, a good theme dictionary will always remain your primary collection of words.

T&P Books' theme-based dictionaries are specialty books that contain the most frequently used words in a language.

The main characteristic of such dictionaries is the division of words into themes. For example, the *City* theme contains the words "street," "crossroads," "square," "fountain," and so on. The *Talking* theme might contain words like "to talk," "to ask," "question," and "answer".

All the words in a theme are divided into smaller units, each comprising 3–5 words. Such an arrangement improves the perception of words and makes the learning process less tiresome. Each unit contains a selection of words with similar meanings or identical roots. This allows you to learn words in small groups and establish other associative links that have a positive effect on memorization.

The words on each page are placed in three columns: a word in your native language, its translation, and its transcription. Such positioning allows for the use of techniques for effective memorization. After closing the translation column, you can flip through and review foreign words, and vice versa. "This is an easy and convenient method of review – one that we recommend you do often."

Our theme-based dictionaries contain transcriptions for all the foreign words. Unfortunately, none of the existing transcriptions are able to convey the exact nuances of foreign pronunciation. That is why we recommend using the transcriptions only as a supplementary learning aid. Correct pronunciation can only be acquired with the help of sound. Therefore our collection includes audio theme-based dictionaries.

The process of learning words using T&P Books' theme-based dictionaries gives you the following advantages:

- You have correctly grouped source information, which predetermines your success at subsequent stages of word memorization
- Availability of words derived from the same root (lazy, lazily, lazybones), allowing you to memorize word units instead of separate words
- Small units of words facilitate the process of establishing associative links needed for consolidation of vocabulary
- You can estimate the number of learned words and hence your level of language knowledge
- The dictionary allows for the creation of an effective and high-quality revision process
- You can revise certain themes several times, modifying the revision methods and techniques
- Audio versions of the dictionaries help you to work out the pronunciation of words and develop your skills of auditory word perception

The T&P Books' theme-based dictionaries are offered in several variants differing in the number of words: 1.500, 3.000, 5.000, 7.000, and 9.000 words. There are also dictionaries containing 15,000 words for some language combinations. Your choice of dictionary will depend on your knowledge level and goals.

We sincerely believe that our dictionaries will become your trusty assistant in learning foreign languages and will allow you to easily acquire the necessary vocabulary.

TABLE OF CONTENTS

PRONUNCIATION GUIDE

T&P phonetic alphabet	Persian example	English example
['] (ayn)	[da'vā] دعوا	voiced pharyngeal fricative
['] (hamza)	[ta'id] تایید	glottal stop
[a]	[ravad] رود	shorter than in ask
[ā]	[ātaš] آتش	calf, palm
[b]	[bānk] بانک	baby, book
[č]	[čand] چند	church, French
[d]	[haštād] هشتاد	day, doctor
[e]	[ešq] عشق	elm, medal
[f]	[fandak] فندک	face, food
[g]	[logo] لوگو	game, gold
[h]	[giyāh] گیاه	home, have
[i]	[jazire] جزیره	shorter than in feet
[j]	[jašn] جشن	joke, general
[k]	[kāj] کاج	clock, kiss
[l]	[limu] لیمو	lace, people
[m]	[mājarā] ماجرا	magic, milk
[n]	[norvež] نروژ	sang, thing
[o]	[golf] گلف	pod, John
[p]	[operā] اپرا	pencil, private
[q]	[lāqar] لاغر	between [g] and [h]
[r]	[raqam] رقم	rice, radio
[s]	[sup] سوپ	city, boss
[š]	[duš] دوش	machine, shark
[t]	[tarjome] ترجمه	tourist, trip
[u]	[niru] نیرو	book
[v]	[varšow] ورشو	very, river
[w]	[rowšan] روشن	vase, winter
[x]	[kāx] کاخ	as in Scots 'loch'
[y]	[biyābān] بیابان	yes, New York
[z]	[zanjir] زنجیر	zebra, please
[ž]	[žuan] ژوئن	forge, pleasure

ABBREVIATIONS
used in the vocabulary

English abbreviations

ab.	-	about
adj	-	adjective
adv	-	adverb
anim.	-	animate
as adj	-	attributive noun used as adjective
e.g.	-	for example
etc.	-	et cetera
fam.	-	familiar
fem.	-	feminine
form.	-	formal
inanim.	-	inanimate
masc.	-	masculine
math	-	mathematics
mil.	-	military
n	-	noun
pl	-	plural
pron.	-	pronoun
sb	-	somebody
sing.	-	singular
sth	-	something
v aux	-	auxiliary verb
vi	-	intransitive verb
vi, vt	-	intransitive, transitive verb
vt	-	transitive verb

BASIC CONCEPTS

Basic concepts. Part 1

1. Pronouns

I, me	man	من
you	to	تو
he, she, it	u	او
we	mā	ما
you (to a group)	šomā	شما
they	ān-hā	آنها

2. Greetings. Salutations. Farewells

Hello! (form.)	salām	سلام
Good morning!	sobh bexeyr	صبح بخیر
Good afternoon!	ruz bexeyr!	روز بخیر!
Good evening!	asr bexeyr	عصربخیر
to say hello	salām kardan	سلام کردن
Hi! (hello)	salām	سلام
greeting (n)	salām	سلام
to greet (vt)	salām kardan	سلام کردن
How are you? (form.)	haletān četowr ast?	حالتان چطور است؟
How are you? (fam.)	četorid?	چطورید؟
What's new?	če xabar?	چه خبر؟
Goodbye!	xodāhāfez	خداحافظ
Bye!	bāy bāy	بای بای
See you soon!	be omid-e didār!	به امید دیدار!
Farewell!	xodāhāfez!	خداحافظ!
to say goodbye	xodāhāfezi kardan	خداحافظی کردن
So long!	tā bezudi!	تا بزودی!
Thank you!	motešakker-am!	متشکرم!
Thank you very much!	besyār motešakker-am!	بسیار متشکرم!
You're welcome	xāheš mikonam	خواهش می کنم
Don't mention it!	tašakkor lāzem nist	تشکر لازم نیست
It was nothing	qābel-i nadārad	قابلی ندارد
Excuse me! (fam.)	bebaxšid!	ببخشید!
to excuse (forgive)	baxšidan	بخشیدن

to apologize (vi)	ozr xāstan	عذر خواستن
My apologies	ozr mixāham	عذرمی خواهم
I'm sorry!	bebaxšid!	ببخشید!
to forgive (vt)	baxšidan	بخشیدن
It's okay! (that's all right)	mohem nist	مهم نیست
please (adv)	lotfan	لطفاً

Don't forget!	farāmuš nakonid!	فراموش نکنید!
Certainly!	albate!	البته!
Of course not!	albate ke neh!	البته که نه!
Okay! (I agree)	besyār xob!	بسیارخوب!
That's enough!	bas ast!	بس است!

3. Cardinal numbers. Part 1

0 zero	sefr	صفر
1 one	yek	یک
2 two	do	دو
3 three	se	سه
4 four	čāhār	چهار

5 five	panj	پنج
6 six	šeš	شش
7 seven	haft	هفت
8 eight	hašt	هشت
9 nine	neh	نه

10 ten	dah	ده
11 eleven	yāzdah	یازده
12 twelve	davāzdah	دوازده
13 thirteen	sizdah	سیزده
14 fourteen	čāhārdah	چهارده

15 fifteen	pānzdah	پانزده
16 sixteen	šānzdah	شانزده
17 seventeen	hefdah	هفده
18 eighteen	hijdah	هیجده
19 nineteen	nuzdah	نوزده

20 twenty	bist	بیست
21 twenty-one	bist-o yek	بیست ویک
22 twenty-two	bist-o do	بیست ودو
23 twenty-three	bist-o se	بیست وسه

30 thirty	si	سی
31 thirty-one	si-yo yek	سی ویک
32 thirty-two	si-yo do	سی ودو
33 thirty-three	si-yo se	سی وسه
40 forty	čehel	چهل
41 forty-one	čehel-o yek	چهل ویک

| 42 forty-two | čehel-o do | چهل ودو |
| 43 forty-three | čehel-o se | چهل وسه |

50 fifty	panjāh	پنجاه
51 fifty-one	panjāh-o yek	پنجاه ویک
52 fifty-two	panjāh-o do	پنجاه ودو
53 fifty-three	panjāh-o se	پنجاه وسه

60 sixty	šast	شصت
61 sixty-one	šast-o yek	شصت ویک
62 sixty-two	šast-o do	شصت ودو
63 sixty-three	šast-o se	شصت وسه

70 seventy	haftād	هفتاد
71 seventy-one	haftād-o yek	هفتاد ویک
72 seventy-two	haftād-o do	هفتاد ودو
73 seventy-three	haftād-o se	هفتاد وسه

80 eighty	haštād	هشتاد
81 eighty-one	haštād-o yek	هشتاد ویک
82 eighty-two	haštād-o do	هشتاد ودو
83 eighty-three	haštād-o se	هشتاد وسه

90 ninety	navad	نود
91 ninety-one	navad-o yek	نود ویک
92 ninety-two	navad-o do	نود ودو
93 ninety-three	navad-o se	نود وسه

4. Cardinal numbers. Part 2

100 one hundred	sad	صد
200 two hundred	devist	دویست
300 three hundred	sisad	سیصد

| 400 four hundred | čāhārsad | چهارصد |
| 500 five hundred | pānsad | پانصد |

600 six hundred	šešsad	ششصد
700 seven hundred	haftsad	هفتصد
800 eight hundred	haštsad	هشتصد
900 nine hundred	nohsad	نهصد

1000 one thousand	hezār	هزار
2000 two thousand	dohezār	دوهزار
3000 three thousand	se hezār	سه هزار
10000 ten thousand	dah hezār	ده هزار
one hundred thousand	sad hezār	صد هزار

| million | milyun | میلیون |
| billion | milyārd | میلیارد |

5. Numbers. Fractions

fraction	kasr	کسر
one half	yek dovvom	یک دوم
one third	yek sevvom	یک سوم
one quarter	yek čāhārom	یک چهارم
one eighth	yek panjom	یک هشتم
one tenth	yek dahom	یک دهم
two thirds	do sevvom	دو سوم
three quarters	se čāhārrom	سه چهارم

6. Numbers. Basic operations

subtraction	tafriq	تفریق
to subtract (vi, vt)	tafriq kardan	تفریق کردن
division	taqsim	تقسیم
to divide (vt)	taqsim kardan	تقسیم کردن
addition	jamʿ	جمع
to add up (vt)	jam' kardan	جمع کردن
to add (vi, vt)	ezāfe kardan	اضافه کردن
multiplication	zarb	ضرب
to multiply (vt)	zarb kardan	ضرب کردن

7. Numbers. Miscellaneous

digit, figure	raqam	رقم
number	adad	عدد
numeral	adadi	عددی
minus sign	manfi	منفی
plus sign	mosbat	مثبت
formula	formul	فرمول
calculation	mohāsebe	محاسبه
to count (vi, vt)	šemordan	شمردن
to count up	mohāsebe kardan	محاسبه کردن
to compare (vt)	moqāyse kardan	مقایسه کردن
How much?	čeqadr?	چقدر؟
sum, total	jamʿ-e kol	جمع کل
result	natije	نتیجه
remainder	bāqimānde	باقیمانده
a few (e.g., ~ years ago)	čand	چند
little (I had ~ time)	kami	کمی
the rest	baqiye	بقیه

| one and a half | yek-o nim | یک و نیم |
| dozen | dojin | دوجین |

in half (adv)	be do qesmat	به دو قسمت
equally (evenly)	be tāsavi	به تساوی
half	nim	نیم
time (three ~s)	daf'e	دفعه

8. The most important verbs. Part 1

to advise (vt)	nasihat kardan	نصیحت کردن
to agree (say yes)	movāfeqat kardan	موافقت کردن
to answer (vi, vt)	javāb dādan	جواب دادن
to apologize (vi)	ozr xāstan	عذر خواستن
to arrive (vi)	residan	رسیدن

to ask (~ oneself)	porsidan	پرسیدن
to ask (~ sb to do sth)	xāstan	خواستن
to be (vi)	budan	بودن

to be afraid	tarsidan	ترسیدن
to be hungry	gorosne budan	گرسنه بودن
to be interested in ...	alāqe dāštan	علاقه داشتن
to be needed	hāmi budan	حامی بودن
to be surprised	mote'ajjeb šodan	متعجب شدن
to be thirsty	tešne budan	تشنه بودن
to begin (vt)	šoru' kardan	شروع کردن
to belong to ...	ta'alloq dāštan	تعلق داشتن
to boast (vi)	be rox kešidan	به رخ کشیدن
to break (split into pieces)	šekastan	شکستن

to call (~ for help)	komak xāstan	کمک خواستن
can (v aux)	tavānestan	توانستن
to catch (vt)	gereftan	گرفتن
to change (vt)	avaz kardan	عوض کردن
to choose (select)	entexāb kardan	انتخاب کردن

to come down (the stairs)	pāyin āmadan	پایین آمدن
to compare (vt)	moqāyse kardan	مقایسه کردن
to complain (vi, vt)	šekāyat kardan	شکایت کردن
to confuse (mix up)	qāti kardan	قاطی کردن
to continue (vt)	edāme dādan	ادامه دادن
to control (vt)	kontorol kardan	کنترل کردن

to cook (dinner)	poxtan	پختن
to cost (vt)	qeymat dāštan	قیمت داشتن
to count (add up)	šemordan	شمردن
to count on ...	hesāb kardan	حساب کردن
to create (vt)	ijād kardan	ایجاد کردن
to cry (weep)	gerye kardan	گریه کردن

9. The most important verbs. Part 2

to deceive (vi, vt)	farib dādan	فریب دادن
to decorate (tree, street)	tazyin kardan	تزیین کردن
to defend (a country, etc.)	defā' kardan	دفاع کردن
to demand (request firmly)	darxāst kardan	درخواست کردن
to dig (vt)	kandan	کندن
to discuss (vt)	bahs kardan	بحث کردن
to do (vt)	anjām dādan	انجام دادن
to doubt (have doubts)	šok dāštan	شک داشتن
to drop (let fall)	andāxtan	انداختن
to enter (room, house, etc.)	vāred šodan	وارد شدن
to excuse (forgive)	baxšidan	بخشیدن
to exist (vi)	vojud dāštan	وجود داشتن
to expect (foresee)	pišbini kardan	پیش بینی کردن
to explain (vt)	touzih dādan	توضیح دادن
to fall (vi)	oftādan	افتادن
to find (vt)	peydā kardan	پیدا کردن
to finish (vt)	be pāyān resāndan	به پایان رساندن
to fly (vi)	parvāz kardan	پرواز کردن
to follow ... (come after)	donbāl kardan	دنبال کردن
to forget (vi, vt)	farāmuš kardan	فراموش کردن
to forgive (vt)	baxšidan	بخشیدن
to give (vt)	dādan	دادن
to give a hint	sarnax dādan	سرنخ دادن
to go (on foot)	raftan	رفتن
to go for a swim	ābtani kardan	آبتنی کردن
to go out (for dinner, etc.)	birun raftan	بیرون رفتن
to guess (the answer)	hads zadan	حدس زدن
to have (vt)	dāštan	داشتن
to have breakfast	sobhāne xordan	صبحانه خوردن
to have dinner	šām xordan	شام خوردن
to have lunch	nāhār xordan	ناهار خوردن
to hear (vt)	šenidan	شنیدن
to help (vt)	komak kardan	کمک کردن
to hide (vt)	penhān kardan	پنهان کردن
to hope (vi, vt)	omid dāštan	امید داشتن
to hunt (vi, vt)	šekār kardan	شکار کردن
to hurry (vi)	ajale kardan	عجله کردن

10. The most important verbs. Part 3

to inform (vt)	āgah kardan	آگاه کردن
to insist (vi, vt)	esrār kardan	اصرار کردن
to insult (vt)	towhin kardan	توهین کردن
to invite (vt)	da'vat kardan	دعوت کردن
to joke (vi)	šuxi kardan	شوخی کردن
to keep (vt)	hefz kardan	حفظ کردن
to keep silent	sāket māndan	ساکت ماندن
to kill (vt)	koštan	کشتن
to know (sb)	šenāxtan	شناختن
to know (sth)	dānestan	دانستن
to laugh (vi)	xandidan	خندیدن
to liberate (city, etc.)	āzād kardan	آزاد کردن
to like (I like ...)	dust dāštan	دوست داشتن
to look for ... (search)	jostoju kardan	جستجو کردن
to love (sb)	dust dāštan	دوست داشتن
to make a mistake	eštebāh kardan	اشتباه کردن
to manage, to run	edāre kardan	اداره کردن
to mean (signify)	ma'ni dāštan	معنی داشتن
to mention (talk about)	zekr kardan	ذکر کردن
to miss (school, etc.)	qāyeb budan	غایب بودن
to notice (see)	motevajjeh šodan	متوجه شدن
to object (vi, vt)	moxalefat kardan	مخالفت کردن
to observe (see)	mošāhede kardan	مشاهده کردن
to open (vt)	bāz kardan	باز کردن
to order (meal, etc.)	sefāreš dādan	سفارش دادن
to order (mil.)	farmān dādan	فرمان دادن
to own (possess)	sāheb budan	صاحب بودن
to participate (vi)	šerekat kardan	شرکت کردن
to pay (vi, vt)	pardāxtan	پرداختن
to permit (vt)	ejāze dādan	اجازه دادن
to plan (vt)	barnāmerizi kardan	برنامه ریزی کردن
to play (children)	bāzi kardan	بازی کردن
to pray (vi, vt)	do'ā kardan	دعا کردن
to prefer (vt)	tarjih dādan	ترجیح دادن
to promise (vt)	qowl dādan	قول دادن
to pronounce (vt)	talaffoz kardan	تلفظ کردن
to propose (vt)	pišnahād dādan	پیشنهاد دادن
to punish (vt)	tanbih kardan	تنبیه کردن

11. The most important verbs. Part 4

| to read (vi, vt) | xāndan | خواندن |
| to recommend (vt) | towsie kardan | توصیه کردن |

to refuse (vi, vt)	rad kardan	رد کردن
to regret (be sorry)	afsus xordan	افسوس خوردن
to rent (sth from sb)	ejāre kardan	اجاره کردن
to repeat (say again)	tekrār kardan	تکرار کردن
to reserve, to book	rezerv kardan	رزرو کردن
to run (vi)	davidan	دویدن
to save (rescue)	najāt dādan	نجات دادن
to say (~ thank you)	goftan	گفتن
to scold (vt)	da'vā kardan	دعوا کردن
to see (vt)	didan	دیدن
to sell (vt)	foruxtan	فروختن
to send (vt)	ferestādan	فرستادن
to shoot (vi)	tirandāzi kardan	تیراندازی کردن
to shout (vi)	faryād zadan	فریاد زدن
to show (vt)	nešān dādan	نشان دادن
to sign (document)	emzā kardan	امضا کردن
to sit down (vi)	nešastan	نشستن
to smile (vi)	labxand zadan	لبخند زدن
to speak (vi, vt)	harf zadan	حرف زدن
to steal (money, etc.)	dozdidan	دزدیدن
to stop (for pause, etc.)	motevaghef šodan	متوقف شدن
to stop (please ~ calling me)	bas kardan	بس کردن
to study (vt)	dars xāndan	درس خواندن
to swim (vi)	šenā kardan	شنا کردن
to take (vt)	bardāštan	برداشتن
to think (vi, vt)	fekr kardan	فکر کردن
to threaten (vt)	tahdid kardan	تهدید کردن
to touch (with hands)	lams kardan	لمس کردن
to translate (vt)	tarjome kardan	ترجمه کردن
to trust (vt)	etminān kardan	اطمینان کردن
to try (attempt)	talāš kardan	تلاش کردن
to turn (e.g., ~ left)	pičidan	پیچیدن
to underestimate (vt)	cast-e kam gereftan	دست کم گرفتن
to understand (vt)	fahmidan	فهمیدن
to unite (vt)	mottahed kardan	متحد کردن
to wait (vt)	montazer budan	منتظر بودن
to want (wish, desire)	xāstan	خواستن
to warn (vt)	hošdār dādan	هشدار دادن
to work (vi)	kār kardan	کار کردن
to write (vt)	neveštan	نوشتن
to write down	neveštan	نوشتن

12. Colors

color	rang	رنگ
shade (tint)	teyf-e rang	طیف رنگ
hue	rangmaye	رنگمایه
rainbow	rangin kamān	رنگین کمان

white (adj)	sefid	سفید
black (adj)	siyāh	سیاه
gray (adj)	xākestari	خاکستری

green (adj)	sabz	سبز
yellow (adj)	zard	زرد
red (adj)	sorx	سرخ

blue (adj)	abi	آبی
light blue (adj)	ābi rowšan	آبی روشن
pink (adj)	surati	صورتی
orange (adj)	nārenji	نارنجی
violet (adj)	banafš	بنفش
brown (adj)	qahve i	قهوه ای

| golden (adj) | talāyi | طلایی |
| silvery (adj) | noqre i | نقره ای |

beige (adj)	baž	بژ
cream (adj)	kerem	کرم
turquoise (adj)	firuze i	فیروزه ای
cherry red (adj)	ālbāluyi	آلبالویی
lilac (adj)	banafš yasi	بنفش یاسی
crimson (adj)	zereški	زرشکی

light (adj)	rowšan	روشن
dark (adj)	tire	تیره
bright, vivid (adj)	rowšan	روشن

colored (pencils)	rangi	رنگی
color (e.g., ~ film)	rangi	رنگی
black-and-white (adj)	siyāh-o sefid	سیاه و سفید
plain (one-colored)	yek rang	یک رنگ
multicolored (adj)	rangārang	رنگارنگ

13. Questions

Who?	če kas-i?	چه کسی؟
What?	če čiz-i?	چه چیزی؟
Where? (at, in)	kojā?	کجا؟
Where (to)?	kojā?	کجا؟
From where?	az kojā?	از کجا؟

When?	če vaqt?	چه وقت؟
Why? (What for?)	čerā?	چرا؟
Why? (~ are you crying?)	čerā?	چرا؟

What for?	barā-ye če?	برای چه؟
How? (in what way)	četor?	چطور؟
What? (What kind of ... ?)	kodām?	کدام؟
Which?	kodām?	کدام؟

To whom?	barā-ye ki?	برای کی؟
About whom?	dar bāre-ye ki?	درباره کی؟
About what?	darbāre-ye či?	درباره چی؟
With whom?	bā ki?	با کی؟

| How many? How much? | čeqadr? | چقدر؟ |
| Whose? | māl-e ki? | مال کی؟ |

14. Function words. Adverbs. Part 1

Where? (at, in)	kojā?	کجا؟
here (adv)	in jā	این جا
there (adv)	ānjā	آنجا

| somewhere (to be) | jā-yi | جایی |
| nowhere (not anywhere) | hič kojā | هیچ کجا |

| by (near, beside) | nazdik | نزدیک |
| by the window | nazdik panjere | نزدیک پنجره |

Where (to)?	kojā?	کجا؟
here (e.g., come ~!)	in jā	این جا
there (e.g., to go ~)	ānjā	آنجا
from here (adv)	az injā	از اینجا
from there (adv)	az ānjā	از آنجا

| close (adv) | nazdik | نزدیک |
| far (adv) | dur | دور |

near (e.g., ~ Paris)	nazdik	نزدیک
nearby (adv)	nazdik	نزدیک
not far (adv)	nazdik	نزدیک

left (adj)	čap	چپ
on the left	dast-e čap	دست چپ
to the left	be čap	به چپ

right (adj)	rāst	راست
on the right	dast-e rāst	دست راست
to the right	be rāst	به راست
in front (adv)	jelo	جلو

front (as adj)	jelo	جلو
ahead (the kids ran ~)	jelo	جلو
behind (adv)	aqab	عقب
from behind	az aqab	از عقب
back (towards the rear)	aqab	عقب
middle	vasat	وسط
in the middle	dar vasat	در وسط
at the side	pahlu	پهلو
everywhere (adv)	hame jā	همه جا
around (in all directions)	atrāf	اطراف
from inside	az daxel	از داخل
somewhere (to go)	jā-yi	جایی
straight (directly)	mostaqim	مستقیم
back (e.g., come ~)	aqab	عقب
from anywhere	az har jā	از هر جا
from somewhere	az yek jā-yi	از یک جایی
firstly (adv)	avvalan	اولاً
secondly (adv)	dumā	دوما
thirdly (adv)	sālesan	ثالثاً
suddenly (adv)	nāgahān	ناگهان
at first (in the beginning)	dar avval	در اول
for the first time	barā-ye avvalin bār	برای اولین بار
long before …	xeyli vaqt piš	خیلی وقت پیش
anew (over again)	az now	از نو
for good (adv)	barā-ye hamiše	برای همیشه
never (adv)	hič vaqt	هیچ وقت
again (adv)	dobāre	دوباره
now (adv)	alān	الان
often (adv)	aqlab	اغلب
then (adv)	ān vaqt	آن وقت
urgently (quickly)	foran	فوراً
usually (adv)	ma'mulan	معمولاً
by the way, …	rāst-i	راستی
possible (that is ~)	momken ast	ممکن است
probably (adv)	ehtemālan	احتمالاً
maybe (adv)	šāyad	شاید
besides …	bealāve	بعلاوه
that's why …	be hamin xāter	به همین خاطر
in spite of …	alāraqm	علیرغم
thanks to …	be lotf	به لطف
what (pron.)	če?	چه؟
that (conj.)	ke	که

something	yek čiz-i	یک چیزی
anything (something)	yek kāri	یک کاری
nothing	hič čiz	هیچ چیز
who (pron.)	ki	کی
someone	yek kas-i	یک کسی
somebody	yek kas-i	یک کسی
nobody	hič kas	هیچ کس
nowhere (a voyage to ~)	hič kojā	هیچ کجا
nobody's	māl-e hičkas	مال هیچ کس
somebody's	har kas-i	هر کسی
so (I'm ~ glad)	xeyli	خیلی
also (as well)	ham	هم
too (as well)	ham	هم

15. Function words. Adverbs. Part 2

Why?	čerā?	چرا؟
for some reason	be dalil-i	به دلیلی
because ...	čon	چون
for some purpose	barā-ye maqsudi	برای مقصودی
and	va	و
or	yā	یا
but	ammā	اما
for (e.g., ~ me)	barā-ye	برای
too (~ many people)	besyār	بسیار
only (exclusively)	faqat	فقط
exactly (adv)	daqiqan	دقیقا
about (more or less)	taqriban	تقریباً
approximately (adv)	taqriban	تقریباً
approximate (adj)	taqribi	تقریبی
almost (adv)	taqriban	تقریباً
the rest	baqiye	بقیه
the other (second)	digar	دیگر
other (different)	digar	دیگر
each (adj)	har	هر
any (no matter which)	har	هر
many, much (a lot of)	ziyād	زیاد
many people	besyāri	بسیاری
all (everyone)	hame	همه
in return for ...	dar avaz	در عوض
in exchange (adv)	dar barābar	در برابر
by hand (made)	dasti	دستی

hardly (negative opinion)	baid ast	بعید است
probably (adv)	ehtemālan	احتمالاً
on purpose (intentionally)	amdan	عمداً
by accident (adv)	tasādofi	تصادفی

very (adv)	besyār	بسیار
for example (adv)	masalan	مثلاً
between	beyn	بین
among	miyān	میان
so much (such a lot)	in qadr	این قدر
especially (adv)	maxsusan	مخصوصاً

Basic concepts. Part 2

16. Weekdays

Monday	došanbe	دوشنبه
Tuesday	se šanbe	سه شنبه
Wednesday	čāhāršanbe	چهارشنبه
Thursday	panj šanbe	پنج شنبه
Friday	jom'e	جمعه
Saturday	šanbe	شنبه
Sunday	yek šanbe	یک شنبه
today (adv)	emruz	امروز
tomorrow (adv)	fardā	فردا
the day after tomorrow	pas fardā	پس فردا
yesterday (adv)	diruz	دیروز
the day before yesterday	pariruz	پریروز
day	ruz	روز
working day	ruz-e kāri	روز کاری
public holiday	ruz-e jašn	روز جشن
day off	ruz-e ta'til	روز تعطیل
weekend	āxar-e hafte	آخر هفته
all day long	tamām-e ruz	تمام روز
the next day (adv)	ruz-e ba'd	روز بعد
two days ago	do ruz-e piš	دو روز پیش
the day before	ruz-e qabl	روز قبل
daily (adj)	ruzāne	روزانه
every day (adv)	har ruz	هر روز
week	hafte	هفته
last week (adv)	hafte-ye gozašte	هفته گذشته
next week (adv)	hafte-ye āyande	هفته آینده
weekly (adj)	haftegi	هفتگی
every week (adv)	har hafte	هر هفته
twice a week	do bār dar hafte	دو بار درهفته
every Tuesday	har sešanbe	هر سه شنبه

17. Hours. Day and night

morning	sobh	صبح
in the morning	sobh	صبح
noon, midday	zohr	ظهر

in the afternoon	ba'd az zohr	بعد ازظهر
evening	asr	عصر
in the evening	asr	عصر
night	šab	شب
at night	šab	شب
midnight	nesfe šab	نصفه شب

second	sānie	ثانیه
minute	daqiqe	دقیقه
hour	sā'at	ساعت
half an hour	nim sā'at	نیم ساعت
a quarter-hour	yek rob'	یک ربع
fifteen minutes	pānzdah daqiqe	پانزده دقیقه
24 hours	šabāne ruz	شبانه روز

sunrise	tolu-'e āftāb	طلوع آفتاب
dawn	sahar	سحر
early morning	sobh-e zud	صبح زود
sunset	qorub	غروب

early in the morning	sobh-e zud	صبح زود
this morning	emruz sobh	امروز صبح
tomorrow morning	fardā sobh	فردا صبح

this afternoon	emruz zohr	امروز ظهر
in the afternoon	ba'd az zohr	بعد ازظهر
tomorrow afternoon	fardā ba'd az zohr	فردا بعد ازظهر

| tonight (this evening) | emšab | امشب |
| tomorrow night | fardā šab | فردا شب |

at 3 o'clock sharp	sar-e sā'at-e se	سر ساعت ۳
about 4 o'clock	nazdik-e sā'at-e čāhār	نزدیک ساعت ۴
by 12 o'clock	nazdik zohr	نزدیک ظهر

in 20 minutes	bist daqiqe-ye digar	۲۰ دقیقه دیگر
in an hour	yek sā'at-e digar	یک ساعت دیگر
on time (adv)	be moqe'	به موقع

a quarter of ...	yek rob' be	یک ربع به
within an hour	yek sā'at-e digar	یک ساعت دیگر
every 15 minutes	har pānzdah daqiqe	هر ۱۵ دقیقه
round the clock	šabāne ruz	شبانه روز

18. Months. Seasons

January	žānvie	ژانویه
February	fevriye	فوریه
March	mārs	مارس
April	āvril	آوریل

May	meh	مه
June	žuan	ژوئن
July	žuiye	ژوئیه
August	owt	اوت
September	septãmbr	سپتامبر
October	oktobr	اکتبر
November	novãmbr	نوامبر
December	desãmr	دسامبر
spring	bahãr	بهار
in spring	dar bahãr	در بهار
spring (as adj)	bahãri	بهاری
summer	tãbestãn	تابستان
in summer	dar tãbestãn	در تابستان
summer (as adj)	tãbestãni	تابستانی
fall	pãyiz	پاییز
in fall	dar pãyiz	در پاییز
fall (as adj)	pãyizi	پاییزی
winter	zemestãn	زمستان
in winter	dar zemestãn	در زمستان
winter (as adj)	zemestãni	زمستانی
month	mãh	ماه
this month	in mãh	این ماه
next month	mãh-e ãyande	ماه آینده
last month	mãh-e gozašte	ماه گذشته
a month ago	yek mãh qabl	یک ماه قبل
in a month (a month later)	yek mãh digar	یک ماه دیگر
in 2 months	do mãh-e digar	۲ ماه دیگر
(2 months later)		
the whole month	tamãm-e mãh	تمام ماه
all month long	tamãm-e mãh	تمام ماه
monthly (~ magazine)	mãhãne	ماهانه
monthly (adv)	mãhãne	ماهانه
every month	har mãh	هر ماه
twice a month	do bãr dar mãh	دو بار درماه
year	sãl	سال
this year	emsãl	امسال
next year	sãl-e ãyande	سال آینده
last year	sãl-e gozašte	سال گذشته
a year ago	yek sãl qabl	یک سال قبل
in a year	yek sãl-e digar	یک سال دیگر
in two years	do sãl-e digar	۲ سال دیگر
the whole year	tamãm-e sãl	تمام سال

all year long	tamām-e sāl	تمام سال
every year	har sāl	هر سال
annual (adj)	sālāne	سالانه
annually (adv)	sālāne	سالانه
4 times a year	čāhār bār dar sāl	چهار بار در سال

date (e.g., today's ~)	tārix	تاریخ
date (e.g., ~ of birth)	tārix	تاریخ
calendar	taqvim	تقویم

half a year	nim sāl	نیم سال
six months	nim sāl	نیم سال
season (summer, etc.)	fasl	فصل
century	qarn	قرن

19. Time. Miscellaneous

time	zamān	زمان
moment	lahze	لحظه
instant (n)	lahze	لحظه
instant (adj)	āni	آنی
lapse (of time)	baxši az zamān	بخشی از زمان
life	zendegi	زندگی
eternity	abadiyat	ابدیت

epoch	asr	عصر
era	dowre	دوره
cycle	čarxe	چرخه
period	dowre	دوره
term (short-~)	mohlat	مهلت

the future	āyande	آینده
future (as adj)	āyande	آینده
next time	daf'e-ye ba'd	دفعه بعد
the past	gozašte	گذشته
past (recent)	gozašte	گذشته
last time	daf'e-ye gozašte	دفعه گذشته

later (adv)	ba'dan	بعداً
after (prep.)	ba'd az	بعد از
nowadays (adv)	aknun	اکنون
now (adv)	alān	الان
immediately (adv)	foran	فوراً
soon (adv)	be zudi	به زودی
in advance (beforehand)	az qabl	از قبل

a long time ago	moddathā piš	مدت ها پیش
recently (adv)	axiran	اخیراً
destiny	sarnevešt	سرنوشت
memories (childhood ~)	xāterāt	خاطرات

archives	āršiv	آرشیو
during …	dar zamān	در زمان
long, a long time (adv)	tulāni	طولانی
not long (adv)	kutāh	کوتاه
early (in the morning)	zud	زود
late (not early)	dir	دیر
forever (for good)	barā-ye hamiše	برای همیشه
to start (begin)	šoru' kardan	شروع کردن
to postpone (vt)	mowkul kardan	موکول کردن
at the same time	ham zamān	هم زمان
permanently (adv)	dāemi	دائمی
constant (noise, pain)	dāemi	دائمی
temporary (adj)	movaqqati	موقتی
sometimes (adv)	gāh-i	گاهی
rarely (adv)	be nodrat	به ندرت
often (adv)	aqlab	اغلب

20. Opposites

rich (adj)	servatmand	ثروتمند
poor (adj)	faqir	فقیر
ill, sick (adj)	bimār	بیمار
well (not sick)	sālem	سالم
big (adj)	bozorg	بزرگ
small (adj)	kučak	کوچک
quickly (adv)	sari'	سریع
slowly (adv)	āheste	آهسته
fast (adj)	sari'	سریع
slow (adj)	āheste	آهسته
glad (adj)	xošhāl	خوشحال
sad (adj)	qamgin	غمگین
together (adv)	bāham	باهم
separately (adv)	jodāgāne	جداگانه
aloud (to read)	boland	بلند
silently (to oneself)	be ārāmi	به آرامی
tall (adj)	boland	بلند
low (adj)	kutāh	کوتاه
deep (adj)	amiq	عمیق
shallow (adj)	sathi	سطحی

| yes | bale | بله |
| no | neh | نه |

| distant (in space) | dur | دور |
| nearby (adj) | nazdik | نزدیک |

| far (adv) | dur | دور |
| nearby (adv) | nazdik | نزدیک |

| long (adj) | derāz | دراز |
| short (adj) | kutāh | کوتاه |

| good (kindhearted) | mehrbān | مهربان |
| evil (adj) | badjens | بدجنس |

| married (adj) | mote'ahhel | متاهل |
| single (adj) | mojarrad | مجرد |

| to forbid (vt) | mamnuʿ kardan | ممنوع کردن |
| to permit (vt) | ejāze dādan | اجازه دادن |

| end | pāyān | پایان |
| beginning | šoruʿ | شروع |

| left (adj) | čap | چپ |
| right (adj) | rāst | راست |

| first (adj) | avvalin | اولین |
| last (adj) | āxarin | آخرین |

| crime | jenāyat | جنایت |
| punishment | mojāzāt | مجازات |

| to order (vt) | farmān dādan | فرمان دادن |
| to obey (vi, vt) | etāʿat kardan | اطاعت کردن |

| straight (adj) | mostaqim | مستقیم |
| curved (adj) | monhani | منحنی |

| paradise | behešt | بهشت |
| hell | jahannam | جهنم |

| to be born | motevalled šodan | متولد شدن |
| to die (vi) | mordan | مردن |

| strong (adj) | nirumand | نیرومند |
| weak (adj) | zaʿif | ضعیف |

old (adj)	kohne	کهنه
young (adj)	javān	جوان
old (adj)	qadimi	قدیمی
new (adj)	jadid	جدید

| hard (adj) | soft | سفت |
| soft (adj) | narm | نرم |

| warm (tepid) | garm | گرم |
| cold (adj) | sard | سرد |

| fat (adj) | čāq | چاق |
| thin (adj) | lāqar | لاغر |

| narrow (adj) | bārik | باریک |
| wide (adj) | vasi' | وسیع |

| good (adj) | xub | خوب |
| bad (adj) | bad | بد |

| brave (adj) | šojā' | شجاع |
| cowardly (adj) | tarsu | ترسو |

21. Lines and shapes

square	morabba'	مربع
square (as adj)	morabba'	مربع
circle	dāyere	دایره
round (adj)	gard	گرد
triangle	mosallas	مثلث
triangular (adj)	mosallasi	مثلثی

oval	beyzi	بیضی
oval (as adj)	beyzi	بیضی
rectangle	mostatil	مستطیل
rectangular (adj)	mostatil	مستطیل

pyramid	heram	هرم
rhombus	lowz-i	لوزی
trapezoid	zuzanaqe	ذوزنقه
cube	moka'ab	مکعب
prism	manšur	منشور

circumference	mohit-e monhani	محیط منحنی
sphere	kare	کره
ball (solid sphere)	kare	کره
diameter	qotr	قطر
radius	šo'ā'	شعاع
perimeter (circle's ~)	mohit	محیط
center	markaz	مرکز

horizontal (adj)	ofoqi	افقی
vertical (adj)	amudi	عمودی
parallel (n)	movāzi	موازی
parallel (as adj)	movāzi	موازی

line	xat	خط
stroke	xat	خط
straight line	xatt-e mostaqim	خط مستقیم
curve (curved line)	monhani	منحنی
thin (line, etc.)	nāzok	نازک
contour (outline)	borun namā	برون نما

intersection	taqāto'	تقاطع
right angle	zāvie-ye qāem	زاویه قائم
segment	qet'e	قطعه
sector	baxš	بخش
side (of triangle)	taraf	طرف
angle	zāvie	زاویه

22. Units of measurement

weight	vazn	وزن
length	tul	طول
width	arz	عرض
height	ertefā'	ارتفاع
depth	omq	عمق
volume	hajm	حجم
area	masāhat	مساحت

gram	garm	گرم
milligram	mili geram	میلی گرم
kilogram	kilugeram	کیلوگرم
ton	ton	تن
pound	pond	پوند
ounce	ons	اونس

meter	metr	متر
millimeter	mili metr	میلی متر
centimeter	sāntimetr	سانتیمتر
kilometer	kilumetr	کیلومتر
mile	māyel	مایل

inch	inč	اینچ
foot	fowt	فوت
yard	yārd	یارد

square meter	metr morabba'	متر مربع
hectare	hektār	هکتار

liter	litr	لیتر
degree	daraje	درجه
volt	volt	ولت
ampere	āmper	آمپر
horsepower	asb-e boxār	اسب بخار
quantity	meqdār	مقدار

a little bit of ...	kami	کمی
half	nim	نیم
dozen	dojin	دوجین
piece (item)	tā	تا
size	andāze	اندازه
scale (map ~)	meqyās	مقیاس
minimal (adj)	haddeaqal	حداقل
the smallest (adj)	kučaktarin	کوچکترین
medium (adj)	motevasset	متوسط
maximal (adj)	haddeaksar	حداکثر
the largest (adj)	bištarin	بیشترین

23. Containers

canning jar (glass ~)	šišeh konserv	شیشه کنسرو
can	quti	قوطی
bucket	satl	سطل
barrel	boške	بشکه
wash basin (e.g., plastic ~)	tašt	تشت
tank (100L water ~)	maxzan	مخزن
hip flask	qomqome	قمقمه
jerrycan	dabbe	دبه
tank (e.g., tank car)	maxzan	مخزن
mug	livān	لیوان
cup (of coffee, etc.)	fenjān	فنجان
saucer	na'lbeki	نعلبکی
glass (tumbler)	estekān	استکان
wine glass	gilās-e šarāb	گیلاس شراب
stock pot (soup pot)	qāblame	قابلمه
bottle (~ of wine)	botri	بطری
neck (of the bottle, etc.)	gardan-e botri	گردن بطری
carafe (decanter)	tong	تنگ
pitcher	pārč	پارچ
vessel (container)	zarf	ظرف
pot (crock, stoneware ~)	sofāl	سفال
vase	goldān	گلدان
bottle (perfume ~)	botri	بطری
vial, small bottle	viyāl	ویال
tube (of toothpaste)	tiyub	تیوب
sack (bag)	kise	کیسه
bag (paper ~, plastic ~)	pākat	پاکت
pack (of cigarettes, etc.)	baste	بسته

box (e.g., shoebox)	ja'be	جعبه
crate	sanduq	صندوق
basket	sabad	سبد

24. Materials

material	mādde	ماده
wood (n)	deraxt	درخت
wood-, wooden (adj)	čubi	چوبی

| glass (n) | šiše | شیشه |
| glass (as adj) | šiše i | شیشه ای |

| stone (n) | sang | سنگ |
| stone (as adj) | sangi | سنگی |

| plastic (n) | pelāstik | پلاستیک |
| plastic (as adj) | pelāstiki | پلاستیکی |

| rubber (n) | lāstik | لاستیک |
| rubber (as adj) | lāstiki | لاستیکی |

| cloth, fabric (n) | pārče | پارچه |
| fabric (as adj) | pārče-i | پارچه ی |

| paper (n) | kāqaz | کاغذ |
| paper (as adj) | kāqazi | کاغذی |

| cardboard (n) | kārton | کارتن |
| cardboard (as adj) | kārtoni | کارتونی |

polyethylene	polietilen	پلیاتیلن
cellophane	solofān	سلوفان
linoleum	linoleom	لینولئوم
plywood	taxte-ye čand lāyi	تخته چند لایی

porcelain (n)	čini	چینی
porcelain (as adj)	čini	چینی
clay (n)	xāk-e ros	خاک رس
clay (as adj)	sofāli	سفالی
ceramic (n)	serāmik	سرامیک
ceramic (as adj)	serāmiki	سرامیکی

25. Metals

metal (n)	felez	فلز
metal (as adj)	felezi	فلزی
alloy (n)	ālyiāž	آلیاژ

gold (n)	talā	طلا
gold, golden (adj)	talā	طلا
silver (n)	noqre	نقره
silver (as adj)	noqre	نقره
iron (n)	āhan	آهن
iron-, made of iron (adj)	āhani	آهنی
steel (n)	fulād	فولاد
steel (as adj)	fulādi	فولادی
copper (n)	mes	مس
copper (as adj)	mesi	مسی
aluminum (n)	ālominiyom	آلومینیوم
aluminum (as adj)	ālominiyomi	آلومینیومی
bronze (n)	boronz	برنز
bronze (as adj)	boronzi	برنزی
brass	berenj	برنج
nickel	nikel	نیکل
platinum	pelātin	پلاتین
mercury	jive	جیوه
tin	qal'	قلع
lead	sorb	سرب
zinc	ruy	روی

HUMAN BEING

Human being. The body

26. Humans. Basic concepts

human being	ensān	انسان
man (adult male)	mard	مرد
woman	zan	زن
child	kudak	کودک
girl	doxtar	دختر
boy	pesar bače	پسر بچه
teenager	nowjavān	نوجوان
old man	pirmard	پیرمرد
old woman	pirzan	پیرزن

27. Human anatomy

organism (body)	orgānism	ارگانیسم
heart	qalb	قلب
blood	xun	خون
artery	sorxrag	سرخرگ
vein	siyāhrag	سیاهرگ
brain	maqz	مغز
nerve	asab	عصب
nerves	a'sāb	اعصاب
vertebra	mohre	مهره
spine (backbone)	sotun-e faqarāt	ستون فقرات
stomach (organ)	me'de	معده
intestines, bowels	rude	روده
intestine (e.g., large ~)	rude	روده
liver	kabed	کبد
kidney	kolliye	کلیه
bone	ostexān	استخوان
skeleton	eskelet	اسکلت
rib	dande	دنده
skull	jomjome	جمجمه
muscle	azole	عضله
biceps	azole-ye dosar	عضلۀ دوسر

triceps	azole-ye se sar	عضلهٔ سه سر
tendon	tāndon	تاندون
joint	mofassal	مفصل
lungs	rie	ریه
genitals	ɛndām hā-ye tanāsol-i	اندام های تناسلی
skin	pust	پوست

28. Head

head	sar	سر
face	surat	صورت
nose	bini	بینی
mouth	dahān	دهان

eye	češm	چشم
eyes	češm-hā	چشم ها
pupil	mardomak	مردمک
eyebrow	abru	ابرو
eyelash	može	مژه
eyelid	pelek	پلک

tongue	zabān	زبان
tooth	dandān	دندان
lips	lab-hā	لب ها
cheekbones	ostexānhā-ye gune	استخوان های گونه
gum	lase	لثه
palate	saqf-e dahān	سقف دهان

nostrils	surāxhā-ye bini	سوراخ های بینی
chin	čāne	چانه
jaw	fak	فک
cheek	gune	گونه

forehead	pišāni	پیشانی
temple	gijgāh	گیجگاه
ear	guš	گوش
back of the head	pas gardan	پس گردن
neck	gardan	گردن
throat	galu	گلو

hair	mu-hā	مو ها
hairstyle	model-e mu	مدل مو
haircut	model-e mu	مدل مو
wig	kolāh-e gis	کلاه گیس

mustache	sebil	سبیل
beard	riš	ریش
to have (a beard, etc.)	gozāštan	گذاشتن
braid	muy-ye bāfte	موی بافته
sideburns	xatt-e riš	خط ریش

red-haired (adj)	muqermez	موقرمز
gray (hair)	sefid-e mu	سفید مو
bald (adj)	tās	طاس
bald patch	tāsi	طاسی

| ponytail | dom-e asbi | دم اسبی |
| bangs | čatri | چتری |

29. Human body

hand	dast	دست
arm	bāzu	بازو
finger	angošt	انگشت
toe	šast-e pā	شصت پا
thumb	šost	شست
little finger	angošt-e kučak	انگشت کوچک
nail	nāxon	ناخن

fist	mošt	مشت
palm	kaf-e dast	کف دست
wrist	moč-e dast	مچ دست
forearm	sā'ed	ساعد
elbow	āranj	آرنج
shoulder	ketf	کتف

leg	pā	پا
foot	pā	پا
knee	zānu	زانو
calf (part of leg)	sāq	ساق
hip	rān	ران
heel	pāšne-ye pā	پاشنهٔ پا

body	badan	بدن
stomach	šekam	شکم
chest	sine	سینه
breast	sine	سینه
flank	pahlu	پهلو
back	pošt	پشت
lower back	kamar	کمر
waist	dur-e kamar	دور کمر

navel (belly button)	nāf	ناف
buttocks	nešiman-e gāh	نشیمن گاه
bottom	bāsan	باسن

beauty mark	xāl	خال
birthmark (café au lait spot)	xāl-e mādarzād	خال مادرزاد
tattoo	xāl kubi	خال کوبی
scar	jā-ye zaxm	جای زخم

Clothing & Accessories

30. Outerwear. Coats

clothes	lebās	لباس
outerwear	lebās-e ru	لباس رو
winter clothing	ebās-e zemestāni	لباس زمستانی
coat (overcoat)	pāltow	پالتو
fur coat	pālto-ye pustin	پالتوی پوستین
fur jacket	kot-e pustin	کت پوستین
down coat	kāpšan	کاپشن
jacket (e.g., leather ~)	kot	کت
raincoat (trenchcoat, etc.)	bārāni	بارانی
waterproof (adj)	zed-e āb	ضد آب

31. Men's & women's clothing

shirt (button shirt)	pirāhan	پیراهن
pants	šalvār	شلوار
jeans	jin	جین
suit jacket	kot	کت
suit	kat-o šalvār	کت و شلوار
dress (frock)	lebās	لباس
skirt	dāman	دامن
blouse	boluz	بلوز
knitted jacket (cardigan, etc.)	eliqe-ye kešbāf	جلیقه کشباف
jacket (of woman's suit)	kot	کت
T-shirt	tey šarr-at	تی شرت
shorts (short trousers)	šalvarak	شلوارک
tracksuit	ebās-e varzeši	لباس ورزشی
bathrobe	̃owle-ye hamām	حوله حمام
pajamas	pižāme	پیژامه
sweater	poliver	پلیور
pullover	poliver	پلیور
vest	jeliqe	جلیقه
tailcoat	kat-e dāman gerd	کت دامن گرد
tuxedo	esmoking	اسموکینگ

uniform	oniform	اونیفورم
workwear	lebās-e kār	لباس کار
overalls	rupuš	روپوش
coat (e.g., doctor's smock)	rupuš	روپوش

32. Clothing. Underwear

underwear	lebās-e zir	لباس زیر
boxers, briefs	šort-e bākser	شورت باکسر
panties	šort-e zanāne	شورت زنانه
undershirt (A-shirt)	zir-e pirāhan-i	زیر پیراهنی
socks	jurāb	جوراب

nightgown	lebās-e xāb	لباس خواب
bra	sine-ye band	سینه بند
knee highs (knee-high socks)	sāq	ساق
pantyhose	jurāb-e šalvāri	جوراب شلواری
stockings (thigh highs)	jurāb-e sāqeboland	جوراب ساقه بلند
bathing suit	māyo	مایو

33. Headwear

hat	kolāh	کلاه
fedora	šāpo	شاپو
baseball cap	kolāh beysbāl	کلاه بیس بال
flatcap	kolāh-e taxt	کلاه تخت

beret	kolāh barre	کلاه بره
hood	kolāh-e bārāni	کلاه بارانی
panama hat	kolāh-e dowre-ye boland	کلاه دوره بلند
knit cap (knitted hat)	kolāh-e bāftani	کلاه بافتنی

headscarf	rusari	روسری
women's hat	kolāh-e zanāne	کلاه زنانه
hard hat	kolāh-e imeni	کلاه ایمنی
garrison cap	kolāh-e pādegān	کلاه پادگان
helmet	kolāh-e imeni	کلاه ایمنی

derby	kolāh-e namadi	کلاه نمدی
top hat	kolāh-e ostovānei	کلاه استوانه ای

34. Footwear

footwear	kafš	کفش
shoes (men's shoes)	putin	پوتین

shoes (women's shoes)	kafš	کفش
boots (e.g., cowboy ~)	čakme	چکمه
slippers	dampāyi	دمپایی
tennis shoes (e.g., Nike ~)	kafš katān-i	کفش کتانی
sneakers (e.g., Converse ~)	kafš katān-i	کفش کتانی
sandals	sandal	صندل
cobbler (shoe repairer)	kaffāš	کفاش
heel	pāšne-ye kafš	پاشنهٔ کفش
pair (of shoes)	yek joft	یک جفت
shoestring	band-e kafš	بند کفش
to lace (vt)	band-e kafš bastan	بند کفش بستن
shoehorn	pāšne keš	پاشنه کش
shoe polish	vāks	واکس

35. Textile. Fabrics

cotton (n)	panbe	پنبه
cotton (as adj)	panbe i	پنبه ای
flax (n)	katān	کتان
flax (as adj)	katāni	کتانی
silk (n)	abrišam	ابریشم
silk (as adj)	abrišami	ابریشمی
wool (n)	pašm	پشم
wool (as adj)	pašmi	پشمی
velvet	maxmal	مخمل
suede	jir	جیر
corduroy	maxmal-e kebriti	مخمل کبریتی
nylon (n)	nāylon	نایلون
nylon (as adj)	nāyloni	نایلونی
polyester (n)	poliester	پلی‌استر
polyester (as adj)	poliester	پلپاستر
leather (n)	čarm	چرم
leather (as adj)	čarmi	چرمی
fur (n)	xaz	خز
fur (e.g., ~ coat)	xaz	خز

36. Personal accessories

gloves	dastkeš	دستکش
mittens	castkeš-e yek angošti	دستکش یک انگشتی

scarf (muffler)	šāl-e gardan	شال گردن
glasses (eyeglasses)	eynak	عینک
frame (eyeglass ~)	qāb	قاب
umbrella	čatr	چتر
walking stick	asā	عصا
hairbrush	bores-e mu	برس مو
fan	bādbezan	بادبزن
tie (necktie)	kerāvāt	کراوات
bow tie	pāpiyon	پاپیون
suspenders	band šalvār	بند شلوار
handkerchief	dastmāl	دستمال
comb	šāne	شانه
barrette	sanjāq-e mu	سنجاق مو
hairpin	sanjāq-e mu	سنجاق مو
buckle	sagak	سگک
belt	kamarband	کمربند
shoulder strap	tasme	تسمه
bag (handbag)	keyf	کیف
purse	keyf-e zanāne	کیف زنانه
backpack	kule pošti	کولۀ پشتی

37. Clothing. Miscellaneous

fashion	mod	مد
in vogue (adj)	mod	مد
fashion designer	tarrāh-e lebas	طراح لباس
collar	yaqe	یقه
pocket	jib	جیب
pocket (as adj)	jibi	جیبی
sleeve	āstin	آستین
hanging loop	band-e āviz	بند آویز
fly (on trousers)	zip	زیپ
zipper (fastener)	zip	زیپ
fastener	sagak	سگک
button	dokme	دکمه
buttonhole	surāx-e dokme	سوراخ دکمه
to come off (ab. button)	kande šodan	کنده شدن
to sew (vi, vt)	duxtan	دوختن
to embroider (vi, vt)	golduzi kardan	گلدوزی کردن
embroidery	golduzi	گلدوزی
sewing needle	suzan	سوزن
thread	nax	نخ
seam	darz	درز

to get dirty (vi)	kasif šodan	کثیف شدن
stain (mark, spot)	lakke	لکه
to crease, crumple (vi)	čoruk šodan	چروک شدن
to tear, to rip (vt)	pāre kardan	پاره کردن
clothes moth	šab parre	شب پره

38. Personal care. Cosmetics

toothpaste	xamir-e dandān	خمیر دندان
toothbrush	mesvāk	مسواک
to brush one's teeth	mesvāk zadan	مسواک زدن
razor	tiq	تیغ
shaving cream	kerem-e riš tarāši	کرم ریش تراشی
to shave (vi)	riš tarāšidan	ریش تراشیدن
soap	sābun	صابون
shampoo	šāmpu	شامپو
scissors	qeyči	قیچی
nail file	sohan-e nāxon	سوهان ناخن
nail clippers	nāxon gir	ناخن گیر
tweezers	mučin	موچین
cosmetics	lavāzem-e ārāyeši	لوازم آرایشی
face mask	māsk	ماسک
manicure	mānikur	مانیکور
to have a manicure	mānikur kardan	مانیکور کردن
pedicure	pedikur	پدیکور
make-up bag	k fe lavāzem-e ārāyeši	کیف لوازم آرایشی
face powder	pudr	پودر
powder compact	ja'be-ye pudr	جعبۀ پودر
blusher	sorxāb	سرخاب
perfume (bottled)	atr	عطر
toilet water (lotion)	atr	عطر
lotion	losiyon	لوسیون
cologne	odkolon	اودکلن
eyeshadow	sāye-ye češm	سایه چشم
eyeliner	medād čašm	مداد چشم
mascara	rimel	ریمل
lipstick	mātik	ماتیک
nail polish, enamel	lāk-e nāxon	لاک ناخن
hair spray	esperey-ye mu	اسپری مو
deodorant	deodyrant	دئودورانت
cream	kerem	کرم
face cream	kerem-e surat	کرم صورت

hand cream	kerem-e dast	کرم دست
anti-wrinkle cream	kerem-e zedd-e čoruk	کرم ضد چروک
day cream	kerem-e ruz	کرم روز
night cream	kerem-e šab	کرم شب
day (as adj)	ruzāne	روزانه
night (as adj)	šab	شب

tampon	tāmpon	تامپن
toilet paper (toilet roll)	kāqaz-e tuālet	کاغذ توالت
hair dryer	sešovār	سشوار

39. Jewelry

jewelry	javāherāt	جواهرات
precious (e.g., ~ stone)	qeymati	قیمتی
hallmark stamp	ayār	عیار

ring	angoštar	انگشتر
wedding ring	halqe	حلقه
bracelet	alangu	النگو

earrings	gušvāre	گوشواره
necklace (~ of pearls)	gardan band	گردن بند
crown	tāj	تاج
bead necklace	gardan band	گردن بند

diamond	almās	الماس
emerald	zomorrod	زمرد
ruby	yāqut	یاقوت
sapphire	yāqut-e kabud	یاقوت کبود
pearl	morvārid	مروارید
amber	kahrobā	کهربا

40. Watches. Clocks

watch (wristwatch)	sā'at-e moči	ساعت مچی
dial	safhe-ye sā'at	صفحهٔ ساعت
hand (of clock, watch)	aqrabe	عقربه
metal watch band	band-e sāat	بند ساعت
watch strap	band-e čarmi	بند چرمی

battery	bātri	باطری
to be dead (battery)	tamām šodan bātri	تمام شدن باتری
to change a battery	bātri avaz kardan	باطری عوض کردن
to run fast	jelo oftādan	جلو افتادن
to run slow	aqab māndan	عقب ماندن
wall clock	sā'at-e divāri	ساعت دیواری
hourglass	sā'at-e šeni	ساعت شنی

sundial	sā'at-e āftābi	ساعت آفتابی
alarm clock	sā'at-e zang dār	ساعت زنگ دار
watchmaker	sā'at sāz	ساعت ساز
to repair (vt)	ta'mir kardan	تعمیر کردن

Food. Nutricion

41. Food

meat	gušt	گوشت
chicken	morq	مرغ
Rock Cornish hen (poussin)	juje	جوجه
duck	ordak	اردک
goose	qāz	غاز
game	gušt-e šekār	گوشت شکار
turkey	gušt-e buqalamun	گوشت بوقلمون
pork	gušt-e xuk	گوشت خوک
veal	gušt-e gusāle	گوشت گوساله
lamb	gušt-e gusfand	گوشت گوسفند
beef	gušt-e gāv	گوشت گاو
rabbit	xarguš	خرگوش
sausage (bologna, pepperoni, etc.)	kālbās	کالباس
vienna sausage (frankfurter)	sosis	سوسیس
bacon	beykon	بیکن
ham	žāmbon	ژامبون
gammon	rān xuk	ران خوک
pâté	pāte	پاته
liver	jegar	جگر
hamburger (ground beef)	hamberger	همبرگر
tongue	zabān	زبان
egg	toxm-e morq	تخم مرغ
eggs	toxm-e morq-ha	تخم مرغ ها
egg white	sefide-ye toxm-e morq	سفیده تخم مرغ
egg yolk	zarde-ye toxm-e morq	زرده تخم مرغ
fish	māhi	ماهی
seafood	qazā-ye daryāyi	غذای دریایی
crustaceans	saxtpustān	سختپوستان
caviar	xāviār	خاویار
crab	xarčang	خرچنگ
shrimp	meygu	میگو
oyster	sadaf-e xorāki	صدف خوراکی
spiny lobster	xarčang-e xārdār	خرچنگ خاردار

octopus	hašt pā	هشت پا
squid	māhi-ye morakkab	ماهی مرکب
sturgeon	māhi-ye xāviar	ماهی خاویار
salmon	māhi-ye salemon	ماهی سالمون
halibut	halibut	هالیبوت
cod	māhi-ye rowqan	ماهی روغن
mackerel	māhi-ye esqumeri	ماهی اسقومری
tuna	tan māhi	تن ماهی
eel	mārmāhi	مارماهی
trout	māhi-ye qezelālā	ماهی قزل آلا
sardine	sārdin	ساردین
pike	ordak māhi	اردک ماهی
herring	māhi-ye šur	ماهی شور
bread	nān	نان
cheese	panir	پنیر
sugar	qand	قند
salt	namak	نمک
rice	berenj	برنج
pasta (macaroni)	mākāroni	ماکارونی
noodles	rešte-ye farangi	رشته فرنگی
butter	kare	کره
vegetable oil	rowqan-e nabāti	روغن نباتی
sunflower oil	rowqan āftābgardān	روغن آفتاب گردان
margarine	mārgārin	مارگارین
olives	zeytun	زیتون
olive oil	rowqan-e zeytun	روغن زیتون
milk	šir	شیر
condensed milk	šir-e čegāl	شیر چگال
yogurt	mās-at	ماست
sour cream	xāme-ye torš	خامهٔ ترش
cream (of milk)	saršir	سرشیر
mayonnaise	māyonez	مایونز
buttercream	xāme	خامه
cereal grains (wheat, etc.)	hobubāt	حبوبات
flour	ārd	آرد
canned food	konserv-hā	کنسرو ها
cornflakes	bereštuk	برشتوک
honey	asal	عسل
jam	morabbā	مربا
chewing gum	ādāms	آدامس

42. Drinks

water	āb	آب
drinking water	āb-e āšāmidani	آب آشامیدنی
mineral water	āb-e ma'dani	آب معدنی
still (adj)	bedun-e gāz	بدون گاز
carbonated (adj)	gāzdār	گازدار
sparkling (adj)	gāzdār	گازدار
ice	yax	یخ
with ice	yax dār	یخ دار
non-alcoholic (adj)	bi alkol	بی الکل
soft drink	nušābe-ye bi alkol	نوشابۀ بی الکل
refreshing drink	nušābe-ye xonak	نوشابۀ خنک
lemonade	limunād	لیموناد
liquors	mašrubāt-e alkoli	مشروبات الکلی
wine	šarāb	شراب
white wine	šarāb-e sefid	شراب سفید
red wine	šarāb-e sorx	شراب سرخ
liqueur	likor	لیکور
champagne	šāmpāyn	شامپاین
vermouth	vermut	ورموت
whiskey	viski	ویسکی
vodka	vodkā	ودکا
gin	jin	جین
cognac	konyāk	کنیاک
rum	araq-e neyšekar	عرق نیشکر
coffee	qahve	قهوه
black coffee	qahve-ye talx	قهوۀ تلخ
coffee with milk	šir-qahve	شیرقهوه
cappuccino	kāpočino	کاپوچینو
instant coffee	qahve-ye fowri	قهوه فوری
milk	šir	شیر
cocktail	kuktel	کوکتل
milkshake	kuktele šir	کوکتل شیر
juice	āb-e mive	آب میوه
tomato juice	āb-e gowjefarangi	آب گوجه فرنگی
orange juice	āb-e porteqāl	آب پرتقال
freshly squeezed juice	āb-e mive-ye taze	آب میوۀ تازه
beer	ābejow	آبجو
light beer	ābejow-ye sabok	آبجوی سبک
dark beer	ābejow-ye tire	آبجوی تیره
tea	čāy	چای

| black tea | čāy-e siyāh | چای سیاه |
| green tea | čāy-e sabz | چای سبز |

43. Vegetables

vegetables	sabzijāt	سبزیجات
greens	sabzi	سبزی
tomato	gowje farangi	گوجه فرنگی
cucumber	xiyār	خیار
carrot	havij	هویج
potato	sib zamini	سیب زمینی
onion	piyāz	پیاز
garlic	sir	سیر
cabbage	kalam	کلم
cauliflower	gol kalam	گل کلم
Brussels sprouts	koll-am boruksel	کلم بروکسل
broccoli	kalam borokli	کلم بروکلی
beetroot	čoqondar	چغندر
eggplant	bādenjān	بادنجان
zucchini	kadu sabz	کدو سبز
pumpkin	kadu tanbal	کدو تنبل
turnip	šalqam	شلغم
parsley	ja'fari	جعفری
dill	šavid	شوید
lettuce	kāhu	کاهو
celery	karafs	کرفس
asparagus	mārčube	مارچوبه
spinach	esfenāj	اسفناج
pea	noxod	نخود
beans	lubiyā	لوبیا
corn (maize)	zorrat	ذرت
kidney bean	lubiyā qermez	لوبیا قرمز
bell pepper	felfel	فلفل
radish	torobče	تربچه
artichoke	kangar farangi	کنگرفرنگی

44. Fruits. Nuts

fruit	mive	میوه
apple	sib	سیب
pear	golābi	گلابی
lemon	limu	لیمو

orange	porteqāl	پرتقال
strawberry (garden ~)	tut-e farangi	توت فرنگی
mandarin	nārengi	نارنگی
plum	ālu	آلو
peach	holu	هلو
apricot	zardālu	زردآلو
raspberry	tamešk	تمشک
pineapple	ānānās	آناناس
banana	mowz	موز
watermelon	hendevāne	هندوانه
grape	angur	انگور
sour cherry	ālbālu	آلبالو
sweet cherry	gilās	گیلاس
melon	xarboze	خربزه
grapefruit	gerip forut	گریپ فوروت
avocado	āvokādo	اووکادو
papaya	pāpāyā	پاپایا
mango	anbe	انبه
pomegranate	anār	انار
redcurrant	angur-e farangi-ye sorx	انگور فرنگی سرخ
blackcurrant	angur-e farangi-ye siyāh	انگور فرنگی سیاه
gooseberry	angur-e farangi	انگور فرنگی
bilberry	zoqāl axte	زغال اخته
blackberry	šāh tut	شاه توت
raisin	kešmeš	کشمش
fig	anjir	انجیر
date	xormā	خرما
peanut	bādām zamin-i	بادام زمینی
almond	bādām	بادام
walnut	gerdu	گردو
hazelnut	fandoq	فندق
coconut	nārgil	نارگیل
pistachios	peste	پسته

45. Bread. Candy

bakers' confectionery (pastry)	širini jāt	شیرینی جات
bread	nān	نان
cookies	biskuit	بیسکوییت
chocolate (n)	šokolāt	شکلات
chocolate (as adj)	šokolāti	شکلاتی
candy (wrapped)	āb nabāt	آب نبات

cake (e.g., cupcake)	nān-e širini	نان شیرینی
cake (e.g., birthday ~)	širini	شیرینی
pie (e.g., apple ~)	keyk	کیک
filling (for cake, pie)	čāšni	چاشنی
jam (whole fruit jam)	morabbā	مربا
marmalade	mārmālād	مارمالاد
waffles	vāfel	وافل
ice-cream	bastani	بستنی
pudding	puding	پودینگ

46. Cooked dishes

course, dish	qazā	غذا
cuisine	qazā	غذا
recipe	dastur-e poxt	دستور پخت
portion	pors	پرس
salad	sālād	سالاد
soup	sup	سوپ
clear soup (broth)	pāye-ye sup	پایه سوپ
sandwich (bread)	sāndevič	ساندویچ
fried eggs	nimru	نیمرو
hamburger (beefburger)	hamberger	همبرگر
beefsteak	esteyk	استیک
side dish	moxallafāt	مخلفات
spaghetti	espāgeti	اسپاگتی
mashed potatoes	pure-ye sibi zamini	پورهٔ سیب زمینی
pizza	pitzā	پیتزا
porridge (oatmeal, etc.)	šurbā	شوربا
omelet	ommol-at	املت
boiled (e.g., ~ beef)	āb paz	آب پز
smoked (adj)	dudi	دودی
fried (adj)	sorx šode	سرخ شده
dried (adj)	xošk	خشک
frozen (adj)	yax zade	یخ زده
pickled (adj)	torši	ترشی
sweet (sugary)	širin	شیرین
salty (adj)	šur	شور
cold (adj)	sard	سرد
hot (adj)	dāq	داغ
bitter (adj)	talx	تلخ
tasty (adj)	xoš mazze	خوش مزه
to cook in boiling water	poxtan	پختن

to cook (dinner)	poxtan	پختن
to fry (vt)	sorx kardan	سرخ کردن
to heat up (food)	garm kardan	گرم کردن
to salt (vt)	namak zadan	نمک زدن
to pepper (vt)	felfel pāšidan	فلفل پاشیدن
to grate (vt)	rande kardan	رنده کردن
peel (n)	pust	پوست
to peel (vt)	pust kandan	پوست کندن

47. Spices

salt	namak	نمک
salty (adj)	šur	شور
to salt (vt)	namak zadan	نمک زدن
black pepper	felfel-e siyāh	فلفل سیاه
red pepper (milled ~)	felfel-e sorx	فلفل سرخ
mustard	xardal	خردل
horseradish	torob-e kuhi	ترب کوهی
condiment	adviye	ادویه
spice	adviye	ادویه
sauce	ses	سس
vinegar	serke	سرکه
anise	rāziyāne	رازیانه
basil	reyhān	ریحان
cloves	mixak	میخک
ginger	zanjefil	زنجفیل
coriander	gešniz	گشنیز
cinnamon	dārčin	دارچین
sesame	konjed	کنجد
bay leaf	barg-e bu	برگ بو
paprika	paprika	پاپریکا
caraway	zire	زیره
saffron	za'ferān	زعفران

48. Meals

food	qazā	غذا
to eat (vi, vt)	xordan	خوردن
breakfast	sobhāne	صبحانه
to have breakfast	sobhāne xordan	صبحانه خوردن
lunch	nāhār	ناهار
to have lunch	nāhār xordan	ناهار خوردن

| dinner | šām | شام |
| to have dinner | šām xordan | شام خوردن |

| appetite | eštehā | اشتها |
| Enjoy your meal! | nuš-e jān | نوش جان |

to open (~ a bottle)	bāz kardan	باز کردن
to spill (liquid)	rixtan	ریختن
to spill out (vi)	rixtan	ریختن

to boil (vi)	jušidan	جوشیدن
to boil (vt)	jušāndan	جوشاندن
boiled (~ water)	jušide	جوشیده

| to chill, cool down (vt) | sard kardan | سرد کردن |
| to chill (vi) | sard šodan | سرد شدن |

| taste, flavor | maze | مزه |
| aftertaste | maze | مزه |

| to slim down (lose weight) | lāqar kardan | لاغر کردن |
| diet | režim | رژیم |

| vitamin | vitāmin | ویتامین |
| calorie | kālori | کالری |

| vegetarian (n) | giyāh xār | گیاه خوار |
| vegetarian (adj) | giyāh xāri | گیاه خواری |

fats (nutrient)	čarbi-hā	چربی ها
proteins	porotein	پروتئین
carbohydrates	karbohidrāt-hā	کربو هیدرات ها

slice (of lemon, ham)	qet'e	قطعه
piece (of cake, pie)	tekke	تکه
crumb	zarre	ذره
(of bread, cake, etc.)		

49. Table setting

spoon	qāšoq	قاشق
knife	kārd	کارد
fork	čangāl	چنگال

| cup (e.g., coffee ~) | fenjān | فنجان |
| plate (dinner ~) | bošqāb | بشقاب |

saucer	na'lbeki	نعلبکی
napkin (on table)	dastmāl	دستمال
toothpick	xelāl-e dandān	خلال دندان

50. Restaurant

restaurant	resturãn	رستوران
coffee house	kãfe	کافه
pub, bar	bãr	بار
tearoom	qahve xãne	قهوه خانه
waiter	pišxedmat	پیشخدمت
waitress	pišxedmat	پیشخدمت
bartender	motesaddi-ye bãr	متصدی بار
menu	meno	منو
wine list	kãrt-e šarãb	کارت شراب
to book a table	miz rezerv kardan	میز رزرو کردن
course, dish	qazã	غذا
to order (meal)	sefãreš dãdan	سفارش دادن
to make an order	sefãreš dãdan	سفارش دادن
aperitif	mašrub-e piš qazã	مشروب پیش غذا
appetizer	piš qazã	پیش غذا
dessert	deser	دسر
check	surat hesãb	صورت حساب
to pay the check	surat-e hesãb rã pardãxtan	صورت حساب را پرداختن
to give change	baqiye rã dãdan	بقیه را دادن
tip	an'ãm	انعام

Family, relatives and friends

51. Personal information. Forms

name (first name)	esm	اسم
surname (last name)	nām-e xānevādegi	نام خانوادگی
date of birth	tārix-e tavallod	تاریخ تولد
place of birth	mahall-e tavallod	محل تولد
nationality	melliyat	ملیت
place of residence	mahall-e sokunat	محل سکونت
country	kešvar	کشور
profession (occupation)	šoql	شغل
gender, sex	jens	جنس
height	qad	قد
weight	vazn	وزن

52. Family members. Relatives

mother	mādar	مادر
father	pedar	پدر
son	pesar	پسر
daughter	doxtar	دختر
younger daughter	doxtar-e kučak	دختر کوچک
younger son	pesar-e kučak	پسر کوچک
eldest daughter	doxtar-e bozorg	دختر بزرگ
eldest son	pesar-e bozorg	پسر بزرگ
brother	barādar	برادر
elder brother	barādar-e bozorg	برادر بزرگ
younger brother	barādar-e kučak	برادر کوچک
sister	xāhar	خواهر
elder sister	xāhar-e bozorg	خواهر بزرگ
younger sister	xāhar-e kučak	خواهر کوچک
cousin (masc.)	pesar 'amu	پسر عمو
cousin (fem.)	doxtar amu	دختر عمو
mom, mommy	māmān	مامان
dad, daddy	bābā	بابا
parents	vāledeyn	والدین
child	kudak	کودک
children	bače-hā	بچه ها

grandmother	mādarbozorg	مادربزرگ
grandfather	pedar-bozorg	پدربزرگ
grandson	nave	نوه
granddaughter	nave	نوه
grandchildren	nave-hā	نوه ها

uncle	amu	عمو
aunt	xāle yā amme	خاله یا عمه
nephew	barādar-zāde	برادرزاده
niece	xāhar-zāde	خواهرزاده

mother-in-law (wife's mother)	mādarzan	مادرزن
father-in-law (husband's father)	pedar-šowhar	پدرشوهر
son-in-law (daughter's husband)	dāmād	داماد
stepmother	nāmādari	نامادری
stepfather	nāpedari	ناپدری
infant	nowzād	نوزاد
baby (infant)	širxār	شیرخوار
little boy, kid	pesar-e kučulu	پسر کوچولو

wife	zan	زن
husband	šowhar	شوهر
spouse (husband)	hamsar	همسر
spouse (wife)	hamsar	همسر

married (masc.)	mote'ahhel	متاهل
married (fem.)	mote'ahhel	متاهل
single (unmarried)	mojarrad	مجرد
bachelor	mojarrad	مجرد
divorced (masc.)	talāq gerefte	طلاق گرفته
widow	bive zan	بیوه زن
widower	bive	بیوه

relative	xišāvand	خویشاوند
close relative	aqvām-e nazdik	اقوام نزدیک
distant relative	aqvām-e dur	اقوام دور
relatives	aqvām	اقوام

orphan (boy or girl)	yatim	یتیم
guardian (of a minor)	qayyem	قیم
to adopt (a boy)	be pesari gereftan	به پسری گرفتن
to adopt (a girl)	be doxtari gereftan	به دختری گرفتن

53. Friends. Coworkers

| friend (masc.) | dust | دوست |
| friend (fem.) | dust | دوست |

friendship	dusti	دوستی
to be friends	dust budan	دوست بودن
buddy (masc.)	rafiq	رفیق
buddy (fem.)	rafiq	رفیق
partner	šarik	شریک
chief (boss)	ra'is	رئیس
superior (n)	ra'is	رئیس
owner, proprietor	sāheb	صاحب
subordinate (n)	zirdast	زیردست
colleague	hamkār	همکار
acquaintance (person)	āšnā	آشنا
fellow traveler	hamsafar	همسفر
classmate	ham kelās	هم کلاس
neighbor (masc.)	hamsāye	همسایه
neighbor (fem.)	hamsāye	همسایه
neighbors	hamsāye-hā	همسایه ها

54. Man. Woman

woman	zan	زن
girl (young woman)	doxtar	دختر
bride	arus	عروس
beautiful (adj)	zibā	زیبا
tall (adj)	qad boland	قد بلند
slender (adj)	xoš andām	خوش اندام
short (adj)	qad kutāh	قد کوتاه
blonde (n)	mu bur	مو بور
brunette (n)	mu siyāh	مو سیاه
ladies' (adj)	zanāne	زنانه
virgin (girl)	bākere	باکره
pregnant (adj)	bārdār	باردار
man (adult male)	mard	مرد
blond (n)	mu bur	مو بور
brunet (n)	mu siyāh	مو سیاه
tall (adj)	qad boland	قد بلند
short (adj)	qad kutāh	قد کوتاه
rude (rough)	xašen	خشن
stocky (adj)	tanumand	تنومند
robust (adj)	tanumand	تنومند
strong (adj)	nirumand	نیرومند
strength	niru	نیرو

stout, fat (adj)	čāq	چاق
swarthy (adj)	sabze ru	سبزه رو
slender (well-built)	xoš andām	خوش اندام
elegant (adj)	barāzande	برازنده

55. Age

age	sen	سن
youth (young age)	javāni	جوانی
young (adj)	javān	جوان

| younger (adj) | kučaktar | کوچکتر |
| older (adj) | bozorgtar | بزرگتر |

young man	mard-e javān	مرد جوان
teenager	nowjavān	نوجوان
guy, fellow	mard	مرد

| old man | pirmard | پیرمرد |
| old woman | pirzan | پیرزن |

adult (adj)	bāleq	بالغ
middle-aged (adj)	miyānsāl	میانسال
elderly (adj)	sālmand	سالمند
old (adj)	mosen	مسن

retirement	mostamerri	مستمری
to retire (from job)	bāznešaste šodan	بازنشسته شدن
retiree	bāznešaste	بازنشسته

56. Children

child	kudak	کودک
children	bače-hā	بچه ها
twins	doqolu	دوقلو

cradle	gahvāre	گهواره
rattle	jeqjeqe	جغجغه
diaper	pušak	پوشک

pacifier	pestānak	پستانک
baby carriage	kāleske	کالسکه
kindergarten	kudakestān	کودکستان
babysitter	parastār bače	پرستار بچه

childhood	kudaki	کودکی
doll	arusak	عروسک
toy	asbāb bāzi	اسباب بازی

construction set (toy)	xāne sāzi	خانه سازی
well-bred (adj)	bā tarbiyat	با تربیت
ill-bred (adj)	bi tarbiyat	بی تربیت
spoiled (adj)	lus	لوس

to be naughty	šeytanat kardan	شیطنت کردن
mischievous (adj)	bāziguš	بازیگوش
mischievousness	šeytāni	شیطانی
mischievous child	šeytān	شیطان

| obedient (adj) | moti' | مطیع |
| disobedient (adj) | sarkeš | سرکش |

docile (adj)	āqel	عاقل
clever (smart)	bāhuš	باهوش
child prodigy	kudak nābeqe	کودک نابغه

57. Married couples. Family life

to kiss (vt)	busidan	بوسیدن
to kiss (vi)	hamdigar rā busidan	همدیگر را بوسیدن
family (n)	xānevāde	خانواده
family (as adj)	xānevādegi	خانوادگی
couple	zoj	زوج
marriage (state)	ezdevāj	ازدواج
hearth (home)	kāšāne	کاشانه
dynasty	selsele	سلسله

| date | qarār | قرار |
| kiss | buse | بوسه |

love (for sb)	ešq	عشق
to love (sb)	dust dāštan	دوست داشتن
beloved	mahbub	محبوب

tenderness	mehrbāni	مهربانی
tender (affectionate)	mehrbān	مهربان
faithfulness	vafā	وفا
faithful (adj)	vafādār	وفادار
care (attention)	tavajjoh	توجه
caring (~ father)	ba molāheze	با ملاحظه

newlyweds	tāze ezdevāj karde	تازه ازدواج کرده
honeymoon	māh-e asal	ماه عسل
to get married (ab. woman)	ezdevāj kardan	ازدواج کردن
to get married (ab. man)	ezdevāj kardan	ازدواج کردن
wedding	arusi	عروسی
golden wedding	panjāhomin sālgard-e arusi	پنجاهمین سالگرد عروسی

anniversary	sālgard	سالگرد
lover (masc.)	ma'šuq	معشوق
mistress (lover)	ma'šuqe	معشوقه
adultery	xiyānat	خیانت
to cheat on ... (commit adultery)	xiyānat kardan	خیانت کردن
jealous (adj)	hasud	حسود
to be jealous	hasud budan	حسود بودن
divorce	talāq	طلاق
to divorce (vi)	talāq gereftan	طلاق گرفتن
to quarrel (vi)	da'vā kardan	دعوا کردن
to be reconciled (after an argument)	āšti kardan	آشتی کردن
together (adv)	bāham	باهم
sex	seks	سکس
happiness	xošbaxti	خوشبختی
happy (adj)	xošbaxt	خوشبخت
misfortune (accident)	badbaxti	بدبختی
unhappy (adj)	badbaxt	بدبخت

Character. Feelings. Emotions

58. Feelings. Emotions

feeling (emotion)	ehsās	احساس
feelings	ehsāsat	احساسات
to feel (vt)	ehsās kardan	احساس کردن
hunger	gorosnegi	گرسنگی
to be hungry	gorosne budan	گرسنه بودن
thirst	tešnegi	تشنگی
to be thirsty	tešne budan	تشنه بودن
sleepiness	xāb āludegi	خواب آلودگی
to feel sleepy	xābālud budan	خواب آلود بودن
tiredness	xastegi	خستگی
tired (adj)	xaste	خسته
to get tired	xaste šodan	خسته شدن
mood (humor)	xolq	خلق
boredom	bi hoselegi	بی حوصلگی
to be bored	hosele sar raftan	حوصله سررفتن
seclusion	guše nešini	گوشه نشینی
to seclude oneself	guše nešini kardan	گوشه نشینی کردن
to worry (make anxious)	negarān kardan	نگران کردن
to be worried	negarān šodan	نگران شدن
worrying (n)	negarāni	نگرانی
anxiety	negarāni	نگرانی
preoccupied (adj)	moztareb	مضطرب
to be nervous	asabi šodan	عصبی شدن
to panic (vi)	vahšat kardan	وحشت کردن
hope	omid	امید
to hope (vi, vt)	omid dāštan	امید داشتن
certainty	etminān	اطمینان
certain, sure (adj)	motmaen	مطمئن
uncertainty	adam-e etminān	عدم اطمینان
uncertain (adj)	nā motmaen	نا مطمئن
drunk (adj)	mast	مست
sober (adj)	hošyār	هوشیار
weak (adj)	za'if	ضعیف
happy (adj)	xošbaxt	خوشبخت
to scare (vt)	tarsāndan	ترساندن

| fury (madness) | qeyz | غیظ |
| rage (fury) | xašm | خشم |

depression	afsordegi	افسردگی
discomfort (unease)	nārāhati	ناراحتی
comfort	āsāyeš	آسایش
to regret (be sorry)	afsus xordan	افسوس خوردن
regret	afsus	افسوس
bad luck	bad šāns-i	بد شانسی
sadness	delxori	دلخوری

shame (remorse)	šarm	شرم
gladness	šādi	شادی
enthusiasm, zeal	eštiyāq	اشتیاق
enthusiast	moštāq	مشتاق
to show enthusiasm	eštiyāq dāštan	اشتیاق داشتن

59. Character. Personality

character	šaxsiyat	شخصیت
character flaw	naqs	نقص
mind, reason	aql	عقل

conscience	vejdān	وجدان
habit (custom)	ādat	عادت
ability (talent)	este'dād	استعداد
can (e.g., ~ swim)	tavānestan	توانستن

patient (adj)	bā howsele	با حوصله
impatient (adj)	bi hosele	بی حوصله
curious (inquisitive)	konjkāv	کنجکاو
curiosity	konjkāvi	کنجکاوی

modesty	forutani	فروتنی
modest (adj)	forutan	فروتن
immodest (adj)	gostāx	گستاخ

laziness	tanbali	تنبلی
lazy (adj)	tanbal	تنبل
lazy person (masc.)	tanbal	تنبل

cunning (n)	mokāri	مکاری
cunning (as adj)	makkār	مکار
distrust	bad gomāni	بد گمانی
distrustful (adj)	bad gomān	بد گمان

generosity	sexāvat	سخاوت
generous (adj)	ba sexāvat	با سخاوت
talented (adj)	bā este'dād	با استعداد
talent	este'dād	استعداد

courageous (adj)	šojā'	شجاع
courage	šojā'at	شجاعت
honest (adj)	sādeq	صادق
honesty	sedāqat	صداقت
careful (cautious)	bā ehtiyāt	با احتیاط
brave (courageous)	bi bāk	بی باک
serious (adj)	jeddi	جدی
strict (severe, stern)	saxt gir	سخت گیر
decisive (adj)	mosammam	مصمم
indecisive (adj)	do del	دو دل
shy, timid (adj)	xejālati	خجالتی
shyness, timidity	xejālat	خجالت
confidence (trust)	e'temād	اعتماد
to believe (trust)	bāvar kardan	باور کردن
trusting (credulous)	zud bāvar	زود باور
sincerely (adv)	sādeqāne	صادقانه
sincere (adj)	sādeq	صادق
sincerity	sedāqat	صداقت
open (person)	sarih	صریح
calm (adj)	ārām	آرام
frank (sincere)	rok	رک
naïve (adj)	sāde lowh	ساده لوح
absent-minded (adj)	sar be havā	سربه هوا
funny (odd)	xande dār	خنده دار
greed	hers	حرص
greedy (adj)	haris	حریص
stingy (adj)	xasis	خسیس
evil (adj)	badjens	بدجنس
stubborn (adj)	lajuj	لجوج
unpleasant (adj)	nāxošāyand	ناخوشایند
selfish person (masc.)	xodxāh	خودخواه
selfish (adj)	xodxāhi	خودخواهی
coward	tarsu	ترسو
cowardly (adj)	tarsu	ترسو

60. Sleep. Dreams

to sleep (vi)	xābidan	خوابیدن
sleep, sleeping	xāb	خواب
dream	royā	رویا
to dream (in sleep)	xāb didan	خواب دیدن
sleepy (adj)	xāb ālud	خواب آلود
bed	taxt-e xāb	تخت خواب

mattress	tošak	تشک
blanket (comforter)	patu	پتو
pillow	bālešt	بالشت
sheet	malāfe	ملافه

insomnia	bi-xābi	بیخوابی
sleepless (adj)	bi xāb	بی خواب
sleeping pill	xāb āvar	خواب آور
to take a sleeping pill	xābāvar xordan	خواب آور خوردن

to feel sleepy	xābālud budan	خواب آلود بودن
to yawn (vi)	xamyāze kešidan	خمیازه کشیدن
to go to bed	be raxtexāb raftan	به رختخواب رفتن
to make up the bed	raxtexāb-e pahn kardan	رختخواب پهن کردن
to fall asleep	xābidan	خوابیدن

nightmare	kābus	کابوس
snore, snoring	xoropof	خروپف
to snore (vi)	xoropof kardan	خروپف کردن

alarm clock	sā'at-e zang dār	ساعت زنگ دار
to wake (vt)	bidār kardan	بیدار کردن
to wake up	bidār šodan	بیدار شدن
to get up (vi)	boland šodan	بلند شدن
to wash up (wash face)	dast-o ru šostan	دست و روشستن

61. Humour. Laughter. Gladness

humor (wit, fun)	šuxi	شوخی
sense of humor	šux ta'bi	شوخ طبعی
to enjoy oneself	šādi kardan	شادی کردن
cheerful (merry)	šād	شاد
merriment (gaiety)	šādi	شادی

smile	labxand	لبخند
to smile (vi)	labxand zadan	لبخند زدن
to start laughing	xandidan	خندیدن

| to laugh (vi) | xandidan | خندیدن |
| laugh, laughter | xande | خنده |

anecdote	latife	لطیفه
funny (anecdote, etc.)	xande dār	خنده دار
funny (odd)	xande dār	خنده دار

to joke (vi)	šuxi kardan	شوخی کردن
joke (verbal)	šuxi	شوخی
joy (emotion)	šādi	شادی
to rejoice (vi)	xošhāl šodan	خوشحال شدن
joyful (adj)	xošhāl	خوشحال

62. Discussion, conversation. Part 1

communication	ertebāt	ارتباط
to communicate	ertebāt dāštan	ارتباط داشتن
conversation	mokāleme	مكالمه
dialog	goftogu	گفتگو
discussion (discourse)	mobāhese	مباحثه
dispute (debate)	mošājere	مشاجره
to dispute	mošājere kardan	مشاجره كردن
interlocutor	ham soxan	هم سخن
topic (theme)	mowzu'	موضوع
point of view	noqte nazar	نقطه نظر
opinion (point of view)	nazar	نظر
speech (talk)	soxanrāni	سخنرانی
discussion (of report, etc.)	mozākere	مذاكره
to discuss (vt)	bahs kardan	بحث كردن
talk (conversation)	goftogu	گفتگو
to talk (to chat)	goftogu kardan	گفتگو كردن
meeting	didār	ديدار
to meet (vi, vt)	molāqāt kardan	ملاقات كردن
proverb	zarb-ol-masal	ضرب المثل
saying	zarb-ol-masal	ضرب المثل
riddle (poser)	mo'ammā	معما
to pose a riddle	mo'ammā matrah kardan	معما مطرح كردن
password	ramz	رمز
secret	rāz	راز
oath (vow)	sowgand	سوگند
to swear (an oath)	sowgand xordan	سوگند خوردن
promise	va'de	وعده
to promise (vt)	qowl dādan	قول دادن
advice (counsel)	nasihat	نصيحت
to advise (vt)	nasihat kardan	نصيحت كردن
to follow one's advice	nasihat-e kasi rā donbāl kardan	نصيحت كسی را دنبال كردن
to listen to ... (obey)	guš kardan	گوش كردن
news	xabar	خبر
sensation (news)	hayajān	هيجان
information (data)	ettelā'āt	اطلاعات
conclusion (decision)	natije	نتيجه
voice	sedā	صدا
compliment	ta'rif	تعريف
kind (nice)	bā mohabbat	با محبت
word	kalame	كلمه
phrase	ebārat	عبارت

answer	javāb	جواب
truth	haqiqat	حقیقت
lie	doruq	دروغ

thought	fekr	فکر
idea (inspiration)	fekr	فکر
fantasy	fāntezi	فانتزی

63. Discussion, conversation. Part 2

respected (adj)	mohtaram	محترم
to respect (vt)	ehterām gozāštan	احترام گذاشتن
respect	ehterām	احترام
Dear ... (letter)	gerāmi	گرامی

| to introduce (sb to sb) | mo'arrefi kardan | معرفی کردن |
| to make acquaintance | āšnā šodan | آشنا شدن |

intention	qasd	قصد
to intend (have in mind)	qasd dāštan	قصد داشتن
wish	ārezu	آرزو
to wish (~ good luck)	ārezu kardan	آرزو کردن

surprise (astonishment)	ta'ajjob	تعجب
to surprise (amaze)	mote'ajjeb kardan	متعجب کردن
to be surprised	mote'ajjeb šodan	متعجب شدن

to give (vt)	dādan	دادن
to take (get hold of)	bardāštan	برداشتن
to give back	bargardāndan	برگرداندن
to return (give back)	pas dādan	پس دادن

to apologize (vi)	ozr xāstan	عذر خواستن
apology	ozr xāhi	عذر خواهی
to forgive (vt)	baxšidan	بخشیدن

to talk (speak)	harf zadan	حرف زدن
to listen (vi)	guš dādan	گوش دادن
to hear out	xub guš dādan	خوب گوش دادن
to understand (vt)	fahmidan	فهمیدن

to show (to display)	nešān dādan	نشان دادن
to look at ...	negāh kardan	نگاه کردن
to call (yell for sb)	sedā kardan	صدا کردن
to distract (disturb)	mozāhem šodan	مزاحم شدن
to disturb (vt)	mozāhem šodan	مزاحم شدن
to pass (to hand sth)	dādan	دادن

| demand (request) | xāheš | خواهش |
| to request (ask) | xāheš kardan | خواهش کردن |

demand (firm request)	taqāzā	تقاضا
to demand (request firmly)	darxāst kardan	درخواست کردن
to tease (call names)	dast endāxtan	دست انداختن
to mock (make fun of)	masxare kardan	مسخره کردن
mockery, derision	masxare	مسخره
nickname	laqab	لقب
insinuation	kenāye	کنایه
to insinuate (imply)	kenāye zadan	کنایه زدن
to mean (vt)	ma'ni dāštan	معنی داشتن
description	towsif	توصیف
to describe (vt)	towsif kardan	توصیف کردن
praise (compliments)	tahsin	تحسین
to praise (vt)	tahsin kardan	تحسین کردن
disappointment	nāomidi	ناامیدی
to disappoint (vt)	nāomid kardan	ناامید کردن
to be disappointed	nāomid šodan	ناامید شدن
supposition	farz	فرض
to suppose (assume)	farz kardan	فرض کردن
warning (caution)	extār	اخطار
to warn (vt)	extār dādan	اخطار دادن

64. Discussion, conversation. Part 3

to talk into (convince)	rāzi kardan	راضی کردن
to calm down (vt)	ārām kardan	آرام کردن
silence (~ is golden)	sokut	سکوت
to be silent (not speaking)	sāket māndan	ساکت ماندن
to whisper (vi, vt)	najvā kardan	نجوا کردن
whisper	najvā	نجوا
frankly, sincerely (adv)	sādeqāne	صادقانه
in my opinion ...	be nazar-e man	به نظرمن
detail (of the story)	joz'iyāt	جزئیات
detailed (adj)	mofassal	مفصل
in detail (adv)	be tafsil	به تفصیل
hint, clue	sarnax	سرنخ
to give a hint	sarnax dādan	سرنخ دادن
look (glance)	nazar	نظر
to have a look	nazar andāxtan	نظر انداختن
fixed (look)	bi harekat	بی حرکت
to blink (vi)	pelk zadan	پلک زدن

| to wink (vi) | češmak zadan | چشمک زدن |
| to nod (in assent) | sar-e tekān dādan | سر تکان دادن |

sigh	āh	آه
to sigh (vi)	āh kešidan	آه کشیدن
to shudder (vi)	larzidan	لرزیدن
gesture	žest	ژست
to touch (one's arm, etc.)	lams kardan	لمس کردن
to seize (e.g., ~ by the arm)	gereftan	گرفتن
to tap (on the shoulder)	zadan	زدن

Look out!	movāzeb bāš!	مواظب باش!
Really?	vāqe'an?	واقعاً؟
Are you sure?	motmaenn-i?	مطمئنی؟
Good luck!	movaffaq bāšid!	موفق باشید!
I see!	albate!	البته!
What a pity!	heyf!	حیف!

65. Agreement. Refusal

consent	movāfeqat	موافقت
to consent (vi)	movāfeqat kardan	موافقت کردن
approval	ta'id	تایید
to approve (vt)	ta'id kardan	تایید کردن
refusal	emtenā'	امتناع
to refuse (vi, vt)	rad kardan	رد کردن

Great!	āli	عالی
All right!	xub	خوب
Okay! (I agree)	besyār xob!	بسیارخوب!

forbidden (adj)	mamnu'	ممنوع
it's forbidden	mamnu' ast	ممنوع است
it's impossible	qeyr-e momken ast	غیر ممکن است
incorrect (adj)	nādorost	نادرست

to reject (~ a demand)	rad kardan	رد کردن
to support (cause, idea)	poštibāni kardan	پشتیبانی کردن
to accept (~ an apology)	qabul kardan	قبول کردن

to confirm (vt)	ta'yid kardan	تآیید کردن
confirmation	ta'yid	تآیید
permission	ejāze	اجازه
to permit (vt)	ejāze dādan	اجازه دادن
decision	tasmim	تصمیم
to say nothing (hold one's tongue)	sokut kardan	سکوت کردن
condition (term)	šart	شرط
excuse (pretext)	bahāne	بهانه

| praise (compliments) | tahsin | تحسین |
| to praise (vt) | tahsin kardan | تحسین کردن |

66. Success. Good luck. Failure

success	movaffaqiyat	موفقیت
successfully (adv)	bā movaffaqiyat	با موفقیت
successful (adj)	movaffaqiyat āmiz	موفقیت آمیز

luck (good luck)	šāns	شانس
Good luck!	movaffaq bāšid!	موفق باشید!
lucky (e.g., ~ day)	šāns	شانس
lucky (fortunate)	xoš šāns	خوش شانس

failure	nākāmi	ناکامی
misfortune	bad šāns-i	بد شانسی
bad luck	bad šāns-i	بد شانسی
unsuccessful (adj)	nā movaffaq	نا موفق
catastrophe	fāje'e	فاجعه

pride	eftexār	افتخار
proud (adj)	maqrur	مغرور
to be proud	eftexār kardan	افتخارکردن

winner	barande	برنده
to win (vi)	piruz šodan	پیروز شدن
to lose (not win)	bāxtan	باختن
try	talāš	تلاش
to try (vi)	talāš kardan	تلاش کردن
chance (opportunity)	šāns	شانس

67. Quarrels. Negative emotions

shout (scream)	faryād	فریاد
to shout (vi)	faryād zadan	فریاد زدن
to start to cry out	faryād zadan	فریاد زدن

quarrel	da'vā	دعوا
to quarrel (vi)	da'vā kardan	دعوا کردن
fight (squabble)	mošājere	مشاجره
to make a scene	janjāl kardan	جنجال کردن
conflict	dargiri	درگیری
misunderstanding	su'-e tafāhom	سوء تفاهم

insult	towhin	توهین
to insult (vt)	towhin kardan	توهین کردن
insulted (adj)	towhin šode	توهین شده
resentment	ranješ	رنجش

| to offend (vt) | ranjāndan | رنجاندن |
| to take offense | ranjidan | رنجیدن |

indignation	xašm	خشم
to be indignant	xašmgin šodan	خشمگین شدن
complaint	šekāyat	شکایت
to complain (vi, vt)	šekāyat kardan	شکایت کردن

apology	ozr xāhi	عذر خواهی
to apologize (vi)	ozr xāstan	عذر خواستن
to beg pardon	ozr xāstan	عذر خواستن

criticism	enteqād	انتقاد
to criticize (vt)	enteqād kardan	انتقاد کردن
accusation	ettehām	اتهام
to accuse (vt)	mottaham kardan	متهم کردن

revenge	enteqām	انتقام
to avenge (get revenge)	enteqām gereftan	انتقام گرفتن
to pay back	talāfi darāvardan	تلافی درآوردن

disdain	tahqir	تحقیر
to despise (vt)	tahqir kardan	تحقیر کردن
hatred, hate	nefrat	نفرت
to hate (vt)	motenaffer budan	متنفر بودن

nervous (adj)	asabi	عصبی
to be nervous	asabi šodan	عصبی شدن
angry (mad)	xašmgin	خشمگین
to make angry	xašmgin kardan	خشمگین کردن

humiliation	tahqir	تحقیر
to humiliate (vt)	tahqir kardan	تحقیر کردن
to humiliate oneself	tahqir šodan	تحقیر شدن

| shock | šok | شوک |
| to shock (vt) | šokke kardan | شوکه کردن |

| trouble (e.g., serious ~) | moškel | مشکل |
| unpleasant (adj) | nāxošāyand | ناخوشایند |

fear (dread)	tars	ترس
terrible (storm, heat)	eftezāh	افتضاح
scary (e.g., ~ story)	vahšatnāk	وحشتناک
horror	vahšat	وحشت
awful (crime, news)	vahšat āvar	وحشت آور

to begin to tremble	larzidan	لرزیدن
to cry (weep)	gerye kardan	گریه کردن
to start crying	gerye sar dādan	گریه سر دادن
tear	ašk	اشک
fault	taqsir	تقصیر

guilt (feeling)	gonāh	گناه
dishonor (disgrace)	ār	عار
protest	e'terāz	اعتراض
stress	fešār	فشار
to disturb (vt)	mozāhem šodan	مزاحم شدن
to be furious	xašmgin budan	خشمگین بودن
mad, angry (adj)	xašmgin	خشمگین
to end (~ a relationship)	qat' kardan	قطع کردن
to swear (at sb)	fohš dādan	فحش دادن
to scare (become afraid)	tarsidan	ترسیدن
to hit (strike with hand)	zadan	زدن
to fight (street fight, etc.)	zad-o-xord kardan	زد و خورد کردن
to settle (a conflict)	hal-o-fasl kardan	حل و فصل کردن
discontented (adj)	nārāzi	ناراضی
furious (adj)	qazabnāk	غضبناک
It's not good!	xub nist!	خوب نیست!
It's bad!	bad ast!	بد است!

Medicine

68. Diseases

sickness	bimāri	بیماری
to be sick	bimār budan	بیمار بودن
health	salāmati	سلامتی

runny nose (coryza)	āb-e rizeš-e bini	آب ریزش بینی
tonsillitis	varam-e lowze	ورم لوزه
cold (illness)	sarmā xordegi	سرما خوردگی
to catch a cold	sarmā xordan	سرما خوردن

bronchitis	boronšit	برنشیت
pneumonia	zātorrie	ذات الریه
flu, influenza	ānfolānzā	آنفولانزا

nearsighted (adj)	nazdik bin	نزدیک بین
farsighted (adj)	durbin	دوربین
strabismus (crossed eyes)	enherāf-e čašm	انحراف چشم
cross-eyed (adj)	luč	لوچ
cataract	āb morvārid	آب مروارید
glaucoma	ab-e siyāh	آب سیاه

stroke	sekte-ye maqzi	سکته مغزی
heart attack	sekte-ye qalbi	سکته قلبی
myocardial infarction	ānfārktus	آنفارکتوس
paralysis	falaji	فلجی
to paralyze (vt)	falj kardan	فلج کردن

allergy	ālerži	آلرژی
asthma	āsm	آسم
diabetes	diyābet	دیابت

toothache	dandān-e dard	دندان درد
caries	pusidegi	پوسیدگی

diarrhea	eshāl	اسهال
constipation	yobusat	یبوست
stomach upset	nārāhati-ye me'de	ناراحتی معده
food poisoning	masmumiyat	مسمومیت
to get food poisoning	masmum šodan	مسموم شدن

arthritis	varam-e mafāsel	ورم مفاصل
rickets	rāšitism	راشیتیسم
rheumatism	romātism	روماتیسم

atherosclerosis	tasallob-e šarāin	تصلب شرائين
gastritis	varam-e me'de	ورم معده
appendicitis	āpāndisit	آپاندیسیت
cholecystitis	e tehāb-e kise-ye safrā	التهاب کیسه صفرا
ulcer	zaxm	زخم
measles	sorxak	سرخک
rubella (German measles)	sorxje	سرخجه
jaundice	yaraqān	یرقان
hepatitis	hepātit	هپاتیت
schizophrenia	šizoferni	شیزوفرنی
rabies (hydrophobia)	hāri	هاری
neurosis	extelāl-e a'sāb	اختلال اعصاب
concussion	zarbe-ye maqzi	ضربه مغزی
cancer	saratān	سرطان
sclerosis	eskeleroz	اسکلروز
multiple sclerosis	≡skeleroz čandgāne	اسکلروز چندگانه
alcoholism	alkolism	الکلیسم
alcoholic (n)	alkoli	الکلی
syphilis	siflis	سیفلیس
AIDS	eydz	ایدز
tumor	tumor	تومور
malignant (adj)	bad xim	بد خیم
benign (adj)	xoš xim	خوش خیم
fever	tab	تب
malaria	mālāriyā	مالاریا
gangrene	qānqāriyā	قانقاریا
seasickness	daryā-zadegi	دریازدگی
epilepsy	sar'	صرع
epidemic	epidemi	اپیدمی
typhus	hasbe	حصبه
tuberculosis	sel	سل
cholera	vabā	وبا
plague (bubonic ~)	tā'un	طاعون

69. Symptoms. Treatments. Part 1

symptom	alāem-e bimāri	علائم بیماری
temperature	damā	دما
high temperature (fever)	tab	تب
pulse	nabz	نبض
dizziness (vertigo)	sargije	سرگیجه
hot (adj)	dāq	داغ

| shivering | ra'še | رعشه |
| pale (e.g., ~ face) | rang paride | رنگ پریده |

cough	sorfe	سرفه
to cough (vi)	sorfe kardan	سرفه کردن
to sneeze (vi)	atse kardan	عطسه کردن
faint	qaš	غش
to faint (vi)	qaš kardan	غش کردن

bruise (hématome)	kabudi	کبودی
bump (lump)	barāmadegi	برآمدگی
to bang (bump)	barxord kardan	برخورد کردن
contusion (bruise)	kuftegi	کوفتگی
to get a bruise	zarb didan	ضرب دیدن

to limp (vi)	langidan	لنگیدن
dislocation	dar raftegi	دررفتگی
to dislocate (vt)	dar raftan	دررفتن
fracture	šekastegi	شکستگی
to have a fracture	dočār-e šekastegi šodan	دچار شکستگی شدن

cut (e.g., paper ~)	boridegi	بریدگی
to cut oneself	boridan	بریدن
bleeding	xunrizi	خونریزی

| burn (injury) | suxtegi | سوختگی |
| to get burned | dočār-e suxtegi šodan | دچار سوختگی شدن |

to prick (vt)	surāx kardan	سوراخ کردن
to prick oneself	surāx kardan	سوراخ کردن
to injure (vt)	āsib resāndan	آسیب رساندن
injury	zaxm	زخم
wound	zaxm	زخم
trauma	zarbe	ضربه

to be delirious	hazyān goftan	هذیان گفتن
to stutter (vi)	loknat dāštan	لکنت داشتن
sunstroke	āftāb-zadegi	آفتاب‌زدگی

70. Symptoms. Treatments. Part 2

| pain, ache | dard | درد |
| splinter (in foot, etc.) | xār | خار |

sweat (perspiration)	araq	عرق
to sweat (perspire)	araq kardan	عرق کردن
vomiting	estefrāq	استفراغ
convulsions	tašannoj	تشنج
pregnant (adj)	bārdār	باردار
to be born	motevalled šodan	متولد شدن

delivery, labor	vazʻ-e haml	وضع حمل
to deliver (~ a baby)	be donyā āvardan	به دنیا آوردن
abortion	seqt-e janin	سقط جنین

breathing, respiration	tanaffos	تنفس
in-breath (inhalation)	estenšāq	استنشاق
out-breath (exhalation)	bāzdam	بازدم
to exhale (breathe out)	bāzdamidan	بازدمیدن
to inhale (vi)	nafas kešidan	نفس کشیدن

disabled person	maʻlul	معلول
cripple	falaj	فلج
drug addict	moʻtād	معتاد

deaf (adj)	kar	کر
mute (adj)	lāl	لال
deaf mute (adj)	kar-o lāl	کر و لال

mad, insane (adj)	divāne	دیوانه
madman (demented person)	divāne	دیوانه
madwoman	divāne	دیوانه
to go insane	divāne šodan	دیوانه شدن

gene	žen	ژن
immunity	masuniyat	مصونیت
hereditary (adj)	mowrusi	موروثی
congenital (adj)	mādarzād	مادرزاد

virus	virus	ویروس
microbe	mikrob	میکروب
bacterium	bākteri	باکتری
infection	ofunat	عفونت

71. Symptoms. Treatments. Part 3

| hospital | bimārestān | بیمارستان |
| patient | bimār | بیمار |

diagnosis	tašxis	تشخیص
cure	moʻāleje	معالجه
medical treatment	darmān	درمان
to get treatment	darmān šodan	درمان شدن
to treat (~ a patient)	moʻāleje kardan	معالجه کردن
to nurse (look after)	parastāri kardan	پرستاری کردن
care (nursing ~)	parastāri	پرستاری

operation, surgery	amal-e jarrāhi	عمل جراحی
to bandage (head, limb)	pānsemān kardan	پانسمان کردن
bandaging	pānsemān	پانسمان

vaccination	vāksināsyon	واکسیناسیون
to vaccinate (vt)	vāksine kardan	واکسینه کردن
injection, shot	tazriq	تزریق
to give an injection	tazriq kardan	تزریق کردن
attack	hamle	حمله
amputation	qatʻ-e ozv	قطع عضو
to amputate (vt)	qatʻ kardan	قطع کردن
coma	komā	کما
to be in a coma	dar komā budan	در کما بودن
intensive care	morāqebat-e viže	مراقبت ویژه
to recover (~ from flu)	behbud yāftan	بهبود یافتن
condition (patient's ~)	hālat	حالت
consciousness	huš	هوش
memory (faculty)	hāfeze	حافظه
to pull out (tooth)	dandān kešidan	دندان کشیدن
filling	por kardan	پر کردن
to fill (a tooth)	por kardan	پر کردن
hypnosis	hipnotizm	هیپنوتیزم
to hypnotize (vt)	hipnotizm kardan	هیپنوتیزم کردن

72. Doctors

doctor	pezešk	پزشک
nurse	parastār	پرستار
personal doctor	pezešk-e šaxsi	پزشک شخصی
dentist	dandān pezešk	دندان پزشک
eye doctor	češm-pezešk	چشم پزشک
internist	pezešk omumi	پزشک عمومی
surgeon	jarrāh	جراح
psychiatrist	ravānpezešk	روانپزشک
pediatrician	pezešk-e kudakān	پزشک کودکان
psychologist	ravānšenās	روانشناس
gynecologist	motexasses-e zanān	متخصص زنان
cardiologist	motexasses-e qalb	متخصص قلب

73. Medicine. Drugs. Accessories

medicine, drug	dāru	دارو
remedy	darmān	درمان
to prescribe (vt)	tajviz kardan	تجویز کردن
prescription	nosxe	نسخه
tablet, pill	qors	قرص

ointment	pomād	پماد
ampule	āmpul	آمپول
mixture	šarbat	شربت
syrup	šarbat	شربت
pill	kapsul	کپسول
powder	pudr	پودر
gauze bandage	bānd	باند
cotton wool	panbe	پنبه
iodine	yod	ید
Band-Aid	časb-e zaxm	چسب زخم
eyedropper	qatre čekān	قطره چکان
thermometer	damāsanj	دماسنج
syringe	sorang	سرنگ
wheelchair	vilčer	ویلچر
crutches	čub zir baqal	چوب زیر بغل
painkiller	mosaken	مسکن
laxative	moshel	مسهل
spirits (ethanol)	alkol	الکل
medicinal herbs	giyāhān-e dāruyi	گیاهان دارویی
herbal (~ tea)	giyāhi	گیاهی

74. Smoking. Tobacco products

tobacco	tutun	توتون
cigarette	sigār	سیگار
cigar	sigār	سیگار
pipe	pip	پیپ
pack (of cigarettes)	baste	بسته
matches	kebrit	کبریت
matchbox	quti-ye kebrit	قوطی کبریت
lighter	fandak	فندک
ashtray	zir-sigāri	زیرسیگاری
cigarette case	quti-ye sigār	قوطی سیگار
cigarette holder	čub-e sigār	چوب سیگار
filter (cigarette tip)	filter	فیلتر
to smoke (vi, vt)	sigār kešidan	سیگار کشیدن
to light a cigarette	sigār rowšan kardan	سیگار روشن کردن
smoking	sigār kešidan	سیگار کشیدن
smoker	sigāri	سیگاری
stub, butt (of cigarette)	tah-e sigār	ته سیگار
smoke, fumes	dud	دود
ash	xākestar	خاکستر

HUMAN HABITAT

City

75. City. Life in the city

city, town	šahr	شهر
capital city	pāytaxt	پایتخت
village	rustā	روستا
city map	naqše-ye šahr	نقشهٔ شهر
downtown	markaz-e šahr	مرکز شهر
suburb	hume-ye šahr	حومهٔ شهر
suburban (adj)	hume-ye šahr	حومهٔ شهر
outskirts	hume	حومه
environs (suburbs)	hume	حومه
city block	mahalle	محله
residential block (area)	mahalle-ye maskuni	محلهٔ مسکونی
traffic	obur-o morur	عبور و مرور
traffic lights	čerāq-e rāhnamā	چراغ راهنما
public transportation	haml-o naql-e šahri	حمل و نقل شهری
intersection	čahārrāh	چهارراه
crosswalk	xatt-e āber-e piyāde	خط عابرپیاده
pedestrian underpass	zir-e gozar	زیر گذر
to cross (~ the street)	obur kardan	عبور کردن
pedestrian	piyāde	پیاده
sidewalk	piyāde row	پیاده رو
bridge	pol	پل
embankment (river walk)	xiyābān-e sāheli	خیابان ساحلی
fountain	češme	چشمه
allée (garden walkway)	bāq rāh	باغ راه
park	pārk	پارک
boulevard	bolvār	بولوار
square	meydān	میدان
avenue (wide street)	xiyābān	خیابان
street	xiyābān	خیابان
side street	kuče	کوچه
dead end	bon bast	بن بست
house	xāne	خانه
building	sāxtemān	ساختمان

skyscraper	āsemānxarāš	آسمان‌خراش
facade	namā	نما
roof	bām	بام
window	panjere	پنجره
arch	tāq-e qowsi	طاق قوسی
column	sotun	ستون
corner	nabš	نبش
store window	vitrin	ویترین
signboard (store sign, etc.)	tāblo	تابلو
poster	poster	پوستر
advertising poster	poster-e tabliqāti	پوستر تبلیغاتی
billboard	bilbord	بیلبورد
garbage, trash	āšqāl	آشغال
trashcan (public ~)	satl-e āšqāl	سطل آشغال
to litter (vi)	kasif kardan	کثیف کردن
garbage dump	jā-ye dafn-e āšqāl	جای دفن آشغال
phone booth	kābin-e telefon	کابین تلفن
lamppost	tir-e barq	تیر برق
bench (park ~)	nimkat	نیمکت
police officer	polis	پلیس
police	polis	پلیس
beggar	gedā	گدا
homeless (n)	bi xānomān	بی خانمان

76. Urban institutions

store	maqāze	مغازه
drugstore, pharmacy	dāruxāne	داروخانه
eyeglass store	eynak foruši	عینک فروشی
shopping mall	markaz-e tejāri	مرکز تجاری
supermarket	supermārket	سوپرمارکت
bakery	nānvāyi	نانوایی
baker	nānvā	نانوا
pastry shop	qannādi	قنادی
grocery store	baqqāli	بقالی
butcher shop	gušt foruši	گوشت فروشی
produce store	sabzi foruši	سبزی فروشی
market	bāzār	بازار
coffee house	kāfe	کافه
restaurant	resturān	رستوران
pub, bar	bār	بار
pizzeria	pitzā-foruši	پیتزا فروشی
hair salon	ārāyešgāh	آرایشگاه

post office	post	پست
dry cleaners	xošk-šuyi	خشک‌شویی
photo studio	ātolye-ye akkāsi	آتلیهٔ عکاسی
shoe store	kafš foruši	کفش فروشی
bookstore	ketāb-foruši	کتاب فروشی
sporting goods store	maqāze-ye varzeši	مغازهٔ ورزشی
clothes repair shop	ta'mir-e lebās	تعمیر لباس
formal wear rental	kerāye-ye lebās	کرایهٔ لباس
video rental store	kerāye-ye film	کرایهٔ فیلم
circus	sirak	سیرک
zoo	bāq-e vahš	باغ وحش
movie theater	sinamā	سینما
museum	muze	موزه
library	ketābxāne	کتابخانه
theater	teātr	تئاتر
opera (opera house)	operā	اپرا
nightclub	kābāre	کاباره
casino	kāzino	کازینو
mosque	masjed	مسجد
synagogue	kenešt	کنشت
cathedral	kelisā-ye jāme'	کلیسای جامع
temple	ma'bad	معبد
church	kelisā	کلیسا
college	anistito	انستیتو
university	dānešgāh	دانشگاه
school	madrese	مدرسه
prefecture	ostāndāri	استانداری
city hall	šahrdāri	شهرداری
hotel	hotel	هتل
bank	bānk	بانک
embassy	sefārat	سفارت
travel agency	āžāns-e jahāngardi	آژانس جهانگردی
information office	daftar-e ettelāāt	دفتر اطلاعات
currency exchange	sarrāfi	صرافی
subway	metro	مترو
hospital	bimārestān	بیمارستان
gas station	pomp-e benzin	پمپ بنزین
parking lot	pārking	پارکینگ

77. Urban transportation

bus	otobus	اتوبوس
streetcar	terāmvā	تراموا
trolley bus	otobus-e barqi	اتوبوس برقی
route (of bus, etc.)	xat	خط
number (e.g., bus ~)	šomāre	شماره
to go by ...	raftan bā	رفتن با
to get on (~ the bus)	savār šodan	سوار شدن
to get off ...	piyāde šodan	پیاده شدن
stop (e.g., bus ~)	stgāh-e otobus	ایستگاه اتوبوس
next stop	istgāh-e ba'di	ایستگاه بعدی
terminus	istgāh-e āxar	ایستگاه آخر
schedule	barnāme	برنامه
to wait (vt)	montazer budan	منتظر بودن
ticket	belit	بلیط
fare	qeymat-e belit	قیمت بلیت
cashier (ticket seller)	sanduqdār	صندوقدار
ticket inspection	kontorol-e belit	کنترل بلیط
ticket inspector	kontorol či	کنترل چی
to be late (for ...)	ta'xir dāštan	تأخیرداشتن
to miss (~ the train, etc.)	az dast dādan	از دست دادن
to be in a hurry	ajale kardan	عجله کردن
taxi, cab	tāksi	تاکسی
taxi driver	rānande-ye tāksi	راننده تاکسی
by taxi	bā tāksi	با تاکسی
taxi stand	istgāh-e tāksi	ایستگاه تاکسی
to call a taxi	tāksi gereftan	تاکسی گرفتن
to take a taxi	tāksi gereftan	تاکسی گرفتن
traffic	obur-o morur	عبور و مرور
traffic jam	terāfik	ترافیک
rush hour	sā'at-e šoluqi	ساعت شلوغی
to park (vi)	pārk kardan	پارک کردن
to park (vt)	pārk kardan	پارک کردن
parking lot	pārking	پارکینگ
subway	metro	مترو
station	istgāh	ایستگاه
to take the subway	bā metro raftan	با مترو رفتن
train	qatār	قطار
train station	is-gāh-e rāh-e āhan	ایستگاه راه آهن

78. Sightseeing

monument	mojassame	مجسمه
fortress	qal'e	قلعه
palace	kāx	کاخ
castle	qal'e	قلعه
tower	borj	برج
mausoleum	ārāmgāh	آرامگاه
architecture	me'māri	معماری
medieval (adj)	qorun-e vasati	قرون وسطی
ancient (adj)	qadimi	قدیمی
national (adj)	melli	ملی
famous (monument, etc.)	mašhur	مشهور
tourist	turist	توریست
guide (person)	rāhnamā-ye tur	راهنمای تور
excursion, sightseeing tour	gardeš	گردش
to show (vt)	nešān dādan	نشان دادن
to tell (vt)	hekāyat kardan	حکایت کردن
to find (vt)	peydā kardan	پیدا کردن
to get lost (lose one's way)	gom šodan	گم شدن
map (e.g., subway ~)	naqše	نقشه
map (e.g., city ~)	naqše	نقشه
souvenir, gift	sowqāti	سوغاتی
gift shop	forušgāh-e sowqāti	فروشگاه سوغاتی
to take pictures	aks gereftan	عکس گرفتن
to have one's picture taken	aks gereftan	عکس گرفتن

79. Shopping

to buy (purchase)	xarid kardan	خرید کردن
purchase	xarid	خرید
to go shopping	xarid kardan	خرید کردن
shopping	xarid	خرید
to be open (ab. store)	bāz budan	باز بودن
to be closed	baste budan	بسته بودن
footwear, shoes	kafš	کفش
clothes, clothing	lebās	لباس
cosmetics	lavāzem-e ārāyeši	لوازم آرایشی
food products	mavādd-e qazāyi	مواد غذایی
gift, present	hedye	هدیه
salesman	forušande	فروشنده
saleswoman	forušande-ye zan	فروشنده زن

check out, cash desk	sanduq	صندوق
mirror	āyene	آینه
counter (store ~)	pišxān	پیشخوان
fitting room	otāq porov	اتاق پرو
to try on	emtehān kardan	امتحان کردن
to fit (ab. dress, etc.)	monāseb budan	مناسب بودن
to like (I like …)	dust dāštan	دوست داشتن
price	qeymat	قیمت
price tag	barčasb-e qeymat	برچسب قیمت
to cost (vt)	qeymat dāštan	قیمت داشتن
How much?	čeqadr?	چقدر؟
discount	taxfif	تخفیف
inexpensive (adj)	arzān	ارزان
cheap (adj)	arzān	ارزان
expensive (adj)	gerān	گران
It's expensive	gerān ast	گران است
rental (n)	kerāye	کرایه
to rent (~ a tuxedo)	kerāye kardan	کرایه کردن
credit (trade credit)	vām	وام
on credit (adv)	xarid-e e'tebāri	خرید اعتباری

80. Money

money	pul	پول
currency exchange	tabdil-e arz	تبدیل ارز
exchange rate	nerx-e arz	نرخ ارز
ATM	xodpardāz	خودپرداز
coin	sekke	سکه
dollar	dolār	دلار
euro	yuro	یورو
lira	lire	لیره
Deutschmark	mārk	مارک
franc	farānak	فرانک
pound sterling	pond-e esterling	پوند استرلینگ
yen	yen	ین
debt	qarz	قرض
debtor	bedehkār	بدهکار
to lend (money)	qarz dādan	قرض دادن
to borrow (vi, vt)	qarz gereftan	قرض گرفتن
bank	bānk	بانک
account	hesāb-e bānki	حساب بانکی
to deposit (vt)	rixtan	ریختن

| to deposit into the account | be hesāb rixtan | به حساب ریختن |
| to withdraw (vt) | az hesāb bardāštan | از حساب برداشتن |

credit card	kārt-e e'tebāri	کارت اعتباری
cash	pul-e naqd	پول نقد
check	ček	چک
to write a check	ček neveštan	چک نوشتن
checkbook	daste-ye ček	دسته چک

wallet	kif-e pul	کیف پول
change purse	kif-e pul	کیف پول
safe	gāvsanduq	گاوصندوق

heir	vāres	وارث
inheritance	mirās	میراث
fortune (wealth)	dārāyi	دارایی

lease	ejāre	اجاره
rent (money)	kerāye-ye xāne	کرایة خانه
to rent (sth from sb)	ejāre kardan	اجاره کردن

price	qeymat	قیمت
cost	arzeš	ارزش
sum	jam'-e kol	جمع کل

to spend (vt)	xarj kardan	خرج کردن
expenses	maxārej	مخارج
to economize (vi, vt)	sarfeju-yi kardan	صرفه جویی کردن
economical	maqrun besarfe	مقرون به صرفه

to pay (vi, vt)	pardāxtan	پرداختن
payment	pardāxt	پرداخت
change (give the ~)	pul-e xerad	پول خرد

tax	māliyāt	مالیات
fine	jarime	جریمه
to fine (vt)	jarime kardan	جریمه کردن

81. Post. Postal service

post office	post	پست
mail (letters, etc.)	post	پست
mailman	nāme resān	نامه رسان
opening hours	sā'athā-ye kāri	ساعت های کاری

letter	nāme	نامه
registered letter	nāme-ye sefāreši	نامه سفارشی
postcard	kārt-e postāl	کارت پستال
telegram	telegrām	تلگرام
package (parcel)	baste posti	بسته پستی

money transfer	havāle	حواله
to receive (vt)	gereftan	گرفتن
to send (vt)	ferestādan	فرستادن
sending	ersāl	ارسال

address	nešāni	نشانی
ZIP code	kod-e posti	کد پستی
sender	ferestande	فرستنده
receiver	girande	گیرنده

| name (first name) | esm | اسم |
| surname (last name) | nām-e xānevādegi | نام خانوادگی |

postage rate	ta'refe	تعرفه
standard (adj)	ādi	عادی
economical (adj)	ādi	عادی

weight	vazn	وزن
to weigh (~ letters)	vazn kardan	وزن کردن
envelope	pākat	پاکت
postage stamp	tambr	تمبر
to stamp an envelope	tamr zadan	تمبر زدن

Dwelling. House. Home

82. House. Dwelling

house	xāne	خانه
at home (adv)	dar xāne	در خانه
yard	hayāt	حیاط
fence (iron ~)	hesār	حصار
brick (n)	ājor	آجر
brick (as adj)	ājori	آجری
stone (n)	sang	سنگ
stone (as adj)	sangi	سنگی
concrete (n)	boton	بتن
concrete (as adj)	botoni	بتنی
new (new-built)	jadid	جدید
old (adj)	qadimi	قدیمی
decrepit (house)	maxrube	مخروبه
modern (adj)	modern	مدرن
multistory (adj)	čandtabaqe	چندطبقه
tall (~ building)	boland	بلند
floor, story	tabaqe	طبقه
single-story (adj)	yek tabaqe	یک طبقه
1st floor	tabaqe-ye pāin	طبقهٔ پائین
top floor	tabaqe-ye bālā	طبقهٔ بالا
roof	bām	بام
chimney	dudkeš	دودکش
roof tiles	saqf-e kazeb	سقف کاذب
tiled (adj)	sofāli	سفالی
attic (storage place)	zir-širvāni	زیرشیروانی
window	panjere	پنجره
glass	šiše	شیشه
window ledge	tāqče-ye panjare	طاقچهٔ پنجره
shutters	kerkere	کرکره
wall	divār	دیوار
balcony	bālkon	بالکن
downspout	nāvdān	ناودان
upstairs (to be ~)	bālā	بالا
to go upstairs	bālā raftan	بالا رفتن

| to come down (the stairs) | pāyin āmadan | پایین آمدن |
| to move (to new premises) | asbābkeši kardan | اسباب کشی کردن |

83. House. Entrance. Lift

entrance	darb-e vorudi	درب ورودی
stairs (stairway)	pellekān	پلکان
steps	pelle-hā	پله ها
banister	narde	نرده
lobby (hotel ~)	lābi	لابی

mailbox	sanduq-e post	صندوق پست
garbage can	zobāle dān	زباله دان
trash chute	šuting zobale	شوتینگ زباله

elevator	āsānsor	آسانسور
freight elevator	bālābar	بالابر
elevator cage	kābin-e āsānsor	کابین آسانسور
to take the elevator	āsānsor gereftan	آسانسور گرفتن

apartment	āpārtemān	آپارتمان
residents (~ of a building)	sākenān	ساکنان
neighbor (masc.)	hamsāye	همسایه
neighbor (fem.)	hamsāye	همسایه
neighbors	hamsāye-hā	همسایه ها

84. House. Doors. Locks

door	darb	درب
gate (vehicle ~)	darvāze	دروازه
handle, doorknob	dastgire-ye dar	دستگیرهٔ در
to unlock (unbolt)	bāz kardan	باز کردن
to open (vt)	bāz kardan	باز کردن
to close (vt)	bastan	بستن

key	kelid	کلید
bunch (of keys)	daste	دسته
to creak (door, etc.)	qežqež kardan	غژغژ کردن
creak	qež qež	غژ غژ
hinge (door ~)	lowlā	لولا
doormat	pādari	پادری

door lock	qofl	قفل
keyhole	surāx kelid	سوراخ کلید
crossbar (sliding bar)	kolun-e dar	کلون در
door latch	čeft	چفت
padlock	qofl	قفل
to ring (~ the door bell)	zang zadan	زنگ زدن

ringing (sound)	zang	زنگ
doorbell	zang-e dar	زنگ در
doorbell button	zang	زنگ
knock (at the door)	dar zadan	درزدن
to knock (vi)	dar zadan	درزدن
code	kod	کد
combination lock	qofl-e ramz dār	قفل رمز دار
intercom	āyfon	آیفون
number (on the door)	pelāk-e manzel	پلاک منزل
doorplate	pelāk	پلاک
peephole	češmi	چشمی

85. Country house

village	rustā	روستا
vegetable garden	jāliz	جالیز
fence	parčin	پرچین
picket fence	hesār	حصار
wicket gate	darvāze	دروازه
granary	anbār	انبار
root cellar	zirzamin	زیرزمین
shed (garden ~)	ālonak	آلونک
well (water)	čāh	چاه
stove (wood-fired ~)	boxāri	بخاری
to stoke the stove	rowšan kardan-e boxāri	روشن کردن بخاری
firewood	hizom	هیزم
log (firewood)	kande-ye čub	کندۀ چوب
veranda	eyvān-e sarpušide	ایوان سرپوشیده
deck (terrace)	terās	تراس
stoop (front steps)	vorudi-e xāne	ورودی خانه
swing (hanging seat)	tāb	تاب

86. Castle. Palace

castle	qal'e	قلعه
palace	kāx	کاخ
fortress	qal'e	قلعه
wall (round castle)	divār	دیوار
tower	borj	برج
keep, donjon	borj-e asli	برج اصلی
portcullis	darb-e kešowyi	درب کشویی
underground passage	rāh-e zirzamini	راه زیرزمینی

moat	xandaq	خندق
chain	zanjir	زنجیر
arrow loop	mazqal	مزغل
magnificent (adj)	mojallal	مجلل
majestic (adj)	bāšokuh	باشکوه
impregnable (adj)	nofoz nāpazir	نفوذ ناپذیر
medieval (adj)	qorun-e vasati	قرون وسطی

87. Apartment

apartment	āpārtemān	آپارتمان
room	otāq	اتاق
bedroom	otāq-e xāb	اتاق خواب
dining room	otāq-e qazāxori	اتاق غذاخوری
living room	mehmānxāne	مهمانخانه
study (home office)	daftar	دفتر
entry room	tālār-e vorudi	تالار ورودی
bathroom (room with a bath or shower)	hammām	حمام
half bath	tuālet	توالت
ceiling	saqf	سقف
floor	kaf	کف
corner	guše	گوشه

88. Apartment. Cleaning

to clean (vi, vt)	tamiz kardan	تمیز کردن
to put away (to stow)	morattab kardan	مرتب کردن
dust	gard	گرد
dusty (adj)	gard ālud	گرد آلود
to dust (vt)	gardgiri kardan	گردگیری کردن
vacuum cleaner	jāru barqi	جارو برقی
to vacuum (vt)	jāru barq-i kešidan	جارو برقی کشیدن
to sweep (vi, vt)	jāru kardan	جارو کردن
sweepings	āšqāl	آشغال
order	nazm	نظم
disorder, mess	bi nazmi	بی نظمی
mop	jāru-ye dastedār	جاروی دسته دار
dust cloth	kohne	کهنه
short broom	jārub	جاروب
dustpan	xāk andāz	خاک انداز

89. Furniture. Interior

furniture	mobl	مبل
table	miz	میز
chair	sandali	صندلی
bed	taxt-e xāb	تخت خواب
couch, sofa	kānāpe	کاناپه
armchair	mobl-e rāhati	مبل راحتی
bookcase	qafase-ye ketāb	قفسه کتاب
shelf	qafase	قفسه
wardrobe	komod	کمد
coat rack (wall-mounted ~)	raxt āviz	رخت آویز
coat stand	čub lebāsi	چوب لباسی
bureau, dresser	komod	کمد
coffee table	miz-e pišdasti	میز پیشدستی
mirror	āyene	آینه
carpet	farš	فرش
rug, small carpet	qāliče	قالیچه
fireplace	šumine	شومینه
candle	šamʿ	شمع
candlestick	šamʿdān	شمعدان
drapes	parde	پرده
wallpaper	kāqaz-e divāri	کاغذ دیواری
blinds (jalousie)	kerkere	کرکره
table lamp	čerāq-e rumizi	چراغ رومیزی
wall lamp (sconce)	čerāq-e divāri	چراغ دیواری
floor lamp	ābāžur	آباژور
chandelier	luster	لوستر
leg (of chair, table)	pāye	پایه
armrest	daste-ye sandali	دستهٔ صندلی
back (backrest)	pošti	پشتی
drawer	kešow	کشو

90. Bedding

bedclothes	raxt-e xāb	رخت خواب
pillow	bālešt	بالشت
pillowcase	rubalešt	روبالشت
duvet, comforter	patu	پتو
sheet	malāfe	ملافه
bedspread	rutaxti	روتختی

91. Kitchen

kitchen	āšpazxāne	آشپزخانه
gas	gāz	گاز
gas stove (range)	ojāgh-e gāz	اجاق گاز
electric stove	ojāgh-e barghi	اجاق برقی
oven	fer	فر
microwave oven	māykrofer	مایکروفر
refrigerator	yaxčāl	یخچال
freezer	fereyzer	فریزر
dishwasher	māšin-e zarfšuyi	ماشین ظرفشویی
meat grinder	čarx-e gušt	چرخ گوشت
juicer	ābmive giri	آبمیوه گیری
toaster	towster	توستر
mixer	maxlut kon	مخلوط کن
coffee machine	qahve sāz	قهوه ساز
coffee pot	qahve juš	قهوه جوش
coffee grinder	āsiyāb-e qahve	آسیاب قهوه
kettle	ketri	کتری
teapot	quri	قوری
lid	sarpuš	سرپوش
tea strainer	čāy sāf kon	چای صاف کن
spoon	qāšoq	قاشق
teaspoon	qāšoq čāy xori	قاشق چای خوری
soup spoon	qāšoq sup xori	قاشق سوپ خوری
fork	čangāl	چنگال
knife	kārd	کارد
tableware (dishes)	zoruf	ظروف
plate (dinner ~)	bošqāb	بشقاب
saucer	na'lbeki	نعلبکی
shot glass	gilās-e vodkā	گیلاس ودکا
glass (tumbler)	estekān	استکان
cup	fenjān	فنجان
sugar bowl	qandān	قندان
salt shaker	namakdān	نمکدان
pepper shaker	felfeldān	فلفلدان
butter dish	zarf-e kare	ظرف کره
stock pot (soup pot)	qāblame	قابلمه
frying pan (skillet)	tābe	تابه
ladle	malāqe	ملاقه
colander	ābkeš	آبکش
tray (serving ~)	sini	سینی

bottle	botri	بطری
jar (glass)	šiše	شیشه
can	quti	قوطی

bottle opener	dar bāz kon	در بازکن
can opener	dar bāz kon	در بازکن
corkscrew	dar bāz kon	در بازکن
filter	filter	فیلتر
to filter (vt)	filter kardan	فیلتر کردن

| trash, garbage (food waste, etc.) | āšqāl | آشغال |
| trash can (kitchen ~) | satl-e zobāle | سطل زباله |

92. Bathroom

bathroom	hammām	حمام
water	āb	آب
faucet	šir	شیر
hot water	āb-e dāq	آب داغ
cold water	āb-e sard	آب سرد

toothpaste	xamir-e dandān	خمیر دندان
to brush one's teeth	mesvāk zadan	مسواک زدن
toothbrush	mesvāk	مسواک

to shave (vi)	riš tarāšidan	ریش تراشیدن
shaving foam	xamir-e eslāh	خمیر اصلاح
razor	tiq	تیغ

to wash (one's hands, etc.)	šostan	شستن
to take a bath	hamām kardan	حمام کردن
shower	duš	دوش
to take a shower	duš gereftan	دوش گرفتن
bathtub	vān hammām	وان حمام
toilet (toilet bowl)	tuālet-e farangi	توالت فرنگی
sink (washbasin)	sink	سینک

| soap | sābun | صابون |
| soap dish | jā sābun | جا صابون |

sponge	abr	ابر
shampoo	šāmpu	شامپو
towel	howle	حوله
bathrobe	howle-ye hamām	حوله حمام

laundry (process)	raxčuyi	لباسشویی
washing machine	māšin-e lebas-šui	ماشین لباسشویی
to do the laundry	šostan-e lebās	شستن لباس
laundry detergent	pudr-e lebas-šui	پودر لباسشویی

93. Household appliances

TV set	televiziyon	تلویزیون
tape recorder	zabt-e sowt	ضبط صوت
VCR (video recorder)	video	ویدئو
radio	rādiyo	رادیو
player (CD, MP3, etc.)	paxš konande	پخش کننده
video projector	video porožektor	ویدئو پروژکتور
home movie theater	sinamā-ye xānegi	سینمای خانگی
DVD player	paxš konande-ye di vi di	پخش کننده دی وی دی
amplifier	āmpli-fāyer	آمپلی فایر
video game console	konsul-e bāzi	کنسول بازی
video camera	durbin-e filmbardāri	دوربین فیلمبرداری
camera (photo)	durbin-e akkāsi	دوربین عکاسی
digital camera	durbin-e dijitāl	دوربین دیجیتال
vacuum cleaner	jāru barqi	جارو برقی
iron (e.g., steam ~)	oto	اتو
ironing board	miz-e otu	میز اتو
telephone	telefon	تلفن
cell phone	telefon-e hamrāh	تلفن همراه
typewriter	māšin-e tahrir	ماشین تحریر
sewing machine	čarx-e xayyāti	چرخ خیاطی
microphone	mikrofon	میکروفون
headphones	guši	گوشی
remote control (TV)	kontorol az rāh-e dur	کنترل از راه دور
CD, compact disc	si-di	سیدی
cassette, tape	kāst	کاست
vinyl record	safhe-ye gerāmāfon	صفحه گرامافون

94. Repairs. Renovation

renovations	ta'mir	تعمیر
to renovate (vt)	ta'mir kardan	تعمیر کردن
to repair, to fix (vt)	ta'mir kardan	تعمیر کردن
to put in order	morattab kardan	مرتب کردن
to redo (do again)	dobāre anjām dādan	دوباره انجام دادن
paint	rang	رنگ
to paint (~ a wall)	rang kardan	رنگ کردن
house painter	naqqāš	نقاش
paintbrush	qalam mu	قلم مو
whitewash	sefid kāri	سفید کاری
to whitewash (vt)	sefid kāri kardan	سفید کاری کردن

wallpaper	kāqaz-e divāri	کاغذ دیواری
to wallpaper (vt)	kāqaz-e divāri kardan	کاغذ دیواری کردن
varnish	lāk	لاک
to varnish (vt)	lāk zadan	لاک زدن

95. Plumbing

water	āb	آب
hot water	āb-e dāq	آب داغ
cold water	āb-e sard	آب سرد
faucet	šir	شیر

drop (of water)	qatre	قطره
to drip (vi)	čakidan	چکیدن
to leak (ab. pipe)	našt kardan	نشت کردن
leak (pipe ~)	našt	نشت
puddle	čāle	چاله

pipe	lule	لوله
valve (e.g., ball ~)	šir-e falake	شیر فلکه
to be clogged up	masdud šodan	مسدود شدن

tools	abzār	ابزار
adjustable wrench	āčār-e farānse	آچار فرانسه
to unscrew (lid, filter, etc.)	bāz kardan	باز کردن
to screw (tighten)	pič kardan	پیچ کردن

to unclog (vt)	lule bāz kardan	لوله باز کردن
plumber	lule keš	لوله کش
basement	zirzamin	زیرزمین
sewerage (system)	fāzelāb	فاضلاب

96. Fire. Conflagration

fire (accident)	ātaš suzi	آتش سوزی
flame	šo'le	شعله
spark	jaraqqe	جرقه
smoke (from fire)	dud	دود
torch (flaming stick)	maš'al	مشعل
campfire	ātaš	آتش

gas, gasoline	benzin	بنزین
kerosene (type of fuel)	naft-e sefid	نفت سفید
flammable (adj)	sutani	سوختنی
explosive (adj)	mavādd-e monfajere	مواد منفجره
NO SMOKING	sigār kešidan mamnu'	سیگار کشیدن ممنوع
safety	amniyat	امنیت
danger	xatar	خطر

dangerous (adj)	xatarnāk	خطرناک
to catch fire	ātaš gereftan	آتش گرفتن
explosion	enfejār	انفجار
to set fire	ātaš zadan	آتش زدن
arsonist	ātaš afruz	آتش افروز
arson	ātaš zadan-e amdi	آتش زدن عمدی
to blaze (vi)	šo'levar budan	شعله ور بودن
to burn (be on fire)	suxtan	سوختن
to burn down	suxtan	سوختن
to call the fire department	ātaš-e nešāni rā xabar kardan	آتش نشانی را خبر کردن
firefighter, fireman	ātaš nešān	آتش نشان
fire truck	māšin-e ātašnešāni	ماشین آتش نشانی
fire department	tim-e ātašnešāni	تیم آتش نشانی
fire truck ladder	nardebān-e ātašnešāni	نردبان آتش نشانی
fire hose	šelang-e ātaš-nešāni	شلنگ آتش نشانی
fire extinguisher	capsul-e ātašnešāni	کپسول آتش نشانی
helmet	kolāh-e imeni	کلاه ایمنی
siren	āžir-e xatar	آژیر خطر
to cry (for help)	faryād zadan	فریاد زدن
to call for help	be komak talabidan	به کمک طلبیدن
rescuer	nejāt-e dahande	نجات دهنده
to rescue (vt)	najāt dādan	نجات دادن
to arrive (vi)	residan	رسیدن
to extinguish (vt)	xāmuš kardan	خاموش کردن
water	āb	آب
sand	šen	شن
ruins (destruction)	xarābe	خرابه
to collapse (building, etc.)	foru rixtan	فرو ریختن
to fall down (vi)	rizeš kardan	ریزش کردن
to cave in (ceiling, floor)	foru rixtan	فرو ریختن
piece of debris	qet'e	قطعه
ash	xākestar	خاکستر
to suffocate (die)	xafe šodan	خفه شدن
to be killed (perish)	košte šodan	کشته شدن

HUMAN ACTIVITIES

Job. Business. Part 1

97. Banking

bank	bānk	بانک
branch (of bank, etc.)	šo'be	شعبه
bank clerk, consultant	mošāver	مشاور
manager (director)	modir	مدیر
bank account	hesāb-e bānki	حساب بانکی
account number	šomāre-ye hesāb	شمارهٔ حساب
checking account	hesāb-e jāri	حساب جاری
savings account	hesāb-e pasandāz	حساب پس انداز
to open an account	hesāb-e bāz kardan	حساب باز کردن
to close the account	hesāb rā bastan	حساب را بستن
to deposit into the account	be hesāb rixtan	به حساب ریختن
to withdraw (vt)	az hesāb bardāštan	از حساب برداشتن
deposit	seporde	سپرده
to make a deposit	seporde gozāštan	سپرده گذاشتن
wire transfer	enteqāl	انتقال
to wire, to transfer	enteqāl dādan	انتقال دادن
sum	jam'-e kol	جمع کل
How much?	čeqadr?	چقدر؟
signature	emzā'	امضاء
to sign (vt)	emzā kardan	امضا کردن
credit card	kārt-e e'tebāri	کارت اعتباری
code (PIN code)	kod	کد
credit card number	šomāre-ye kārt-e e'tebāri	شماره کارت اعتباری
ATM	xodpardāz	خودپرداز
check	ček	چک
to write a check	ček neveštan	چک نوشتن
checkbook	daste-ye ček	دسته چک
loan (bank ~)	e'tebār	اعتبار
to apply for a loan	darxāst-e vam kardan	درخواست وام کردن
to get a loan	vām gereftan	وام گرفتن

| to give a loan | vām dādan | وام دادن |
| guarantee | zemānat | ضمانت |

98. Telephone. Phone conversation

telephone	telefon	تلفن
cell phone	telefon-e hamrāh	تلفن همراه
answering machine	monši-ye telefoni	منشی تلفنی
to call (by phone)	telefon zadan	تلفن زدن
phone call	tamās-e telefoni	تماس تلفنی
to dial a number	šomāre gereftan	شماره گرفتن
Hello!	alo!	الو!
to ask (vt)	porsidan	پرسیدن
to answer (vi, vt)	javāb dādan	جواب دادن
to hear (vt)	šenidan	شنیدن
well (adv)	xub	خوب
not well (adv)	bad	بد
noises (interference)	sedā	صدا
receiver	guši	گوشی
to pick up (~ the phone)	guši rā bar dāštan	گوشی را برداشتن
to hang up (~ the phone)	guši rā gozāštan	گوشی را گذاشتن
busy (engaged)	mašqul	مشغول
to ring (ab. phone)	zang zadan	زنگ زدن
telephone book	daftar-e telefon	دفتر تلفن
local (adj)	mahalli	محلی
local call	telefon-e dāxeli	تلفن داخلی
long distance (~ call)	beyn-e šahri	بین شهری
long-distance call	telefon-e beyn-e šahri	تلفن بین شهری
international (adj)	beynolmelali	بین المللی
international call	telefon-e beynolmelali	تلفن بین المللی

99. Cell phone

cell phone	telefon-e hamrāh	تلفن همراه
display	namāyešgar	نمایشگر
button	dokme	دکمه
SIM card	sim-e kārt	سیم کارت
battery	bātri	باطری
to be dead (battery)	tamām šodan bātri	تمام شدن باتری
charger	šāržer	شارژ
menu	meno	منو

settings	tanzimāt	تنظیمات
tune (melody)	āhang	آهنگ
to select (vt)	entexāb kardan	انتخاب کردن
calculator	māšin-e hesāb	ماشین حساب
voice mail	monši-ye telefoni	منشی تلفنی
alarm clock	sā'at-e zang dār	ساعت زنگ دار
contacts	daftar-e telefon	دفتر تلفن
SMS (text message)	payāmak	پیامک
subscriber	moštarek	مشترک

100. Stationery

ballpoint pen	xodkār	خودکار
fountain pen	xodnevis	خودنویس
pencil	medād	مداد
highlighter	māžik	ماژیک
felt-tip pen	māžik	ماژیک
notepad	daftar-e yāddāšt	دفتر یادداشت
agenda (diary)	daftar-e yāddāšt	دفتر یادداشت
ruler	xat keš	خط کش
calculator	māšin-e hesāb	ماشین حساب
eraser	pāk kon	پاک کن
thumbtack	punez	پونز
paper clip	gire	گیره
glue	časb	چسب
stapler	mangane-ye zan	منگنه زن
hole punch	pānč	پانچ
pencil sharpener	madād-e tarāš	مداد تراش

Job. Business. Part 2

101. Mass Media

newspaper	ruznāme	روزنامه
magazine	majalle	مجله
press (printed media)	matbuāt	مطبوعات
radio	rādiyo	رادیو
radio station	istgāh-e rādiyoyi	ایستگاه رادیویی
television	televiziyon	تلویزیون
presenter, host	mojri	مجری
newscaster	guyande-ye axbār	گوینده اخبار
commentator	mofasser	مفسر
journalist	ruznāme negār	روزنامه نگار
correspondent (reporter)	xabarnegār	خبرنگار
press photographer	akkās-e matbuāti	عکاس مطبوعاتی
reporter	gozārešgar	گزارشگر
editor	virāstār	ویراستار
editor-in-chief	sardabir	سردبیر
to subscribe (to ...)	moštarak šodan	مشترک شدن
subscription	ešterāk	اشتراک
subscriber	moštarek	مشترک
to read (vi, vt)	xāndan	خواندن
reader	xānande	خواننده
circulation (of newspaper)	tirāž	تیراژ
monthly (adj)	māhāne	ماهانه
weekly (adj)	haftegi	هفتگی
issue (edition)	šomāre	شماره
new (~ issue)	tāze	تازه
headline	sar xat-e xabar	سرخط خبر
short article	maqāle-ye kutāh	مقاله کوتاه
column (regular article)	sotun	ستون
article	maqāle	مقاله
page	safhe	صفحه
reportage, report	gozāreš	گزارش
event (happening)	vāqe'e	واقعه
sensation (news)	hayajān	هیجان
scandal	janjāl	جنجال
scandalous (adj)	janjāl āvar	جنجال آور

great (~ scandal)	bozorg	بزرگ
show (e.g., cooking ~)	barnāme	برنامه
interview	mosāhebe	مصاحبه
live broadcast	paxš-e mostaqim	پخش مستقیم
channel	kānāl	کانال

102. Agriculture

agriculture	kešāvarzi	کشاورزی
peasant (masc.)	dehqān	دهقان
peasant (fem.)	dehqān	دهقان
farmer	kešāvarz	کشاورز
tractor (farm ~)	terāktor	تراکتور
combine, harvester	kombāyn	کمباین
plow	gāvāhan	گاوآهن
to plow (vi, vt)	šoxm zadan	شخم زدن
plowland	zamin āmāde kešt	زمین آماده کشت
furrow (in field)	šiyār	شیار
to sow (vi, vt)	kāštan	کاشتن
seeder	bazrpāš	بذرپاش
sowing (process)	košt	کشت
scythe	dās	داس
to mow, to scythe	dero kardan	درو کردن
spade (tool)	bil	بیل
to till (vt)	kandan	کندن
hoe	kaj bil	کج بیل
to hoe, to weed	vajin kardan	وجین کردن
weed (plant)	alaf-e harz	علف هرز
watering can	āb pāš	آب پاش
to water (plants)	āb dādan	آب دادن
watering (act)	ābyāri	آبیاری
pitchfork	čangak	چنگک
rake	šen keš	شن کش
fertilizer	kud	کود
to fertilize (vt)	kud dādan	کود دادن
manure (fertilizer)	kud-e heyvāni	کود حیوانی
field	sahrā	صحرا
meadow	čaman	چمن
vegetable garden	jāliz	جالیز
orchard (e.g., apple ~)	bāq	باغ

to graze (vt)	čerāndan	چراندن
herder (herdsman)	čupān	چوپان
pasture	čerā-gāh	چراگاه

| cattle breeding | dāmparvari | دامپروری |
| sheep farming | gusfand dāri | گوسفند داری |

plantation	mazrae	مزرعه
row (garden bed ~s)	radif	ردیف
hothouse	golxāne	گلخانه

| drought (lack of rain) | xošksāli | خشکسالی |
| dry (~ summer) | xošk | خشک |

grain	dāne	دانه
cereal crops	qallāt	غلات
to harvest, to gather	mahsul-e jam' kardan	محصول جمع کردن

miller (person)	āsiyābān	آسیابان
mill (e.g., gristmill)	āsiyāb	آسیاب
to grind (grain)	qalle kubidan	غله کوبیدن
flour	ārd	آرد
straw	kāh	کاه

103. Building. Building process

construction site	mahal-e sāxt-o sāz	محل ساخت و ساز
to build (vt)	sāxtan	ساختن
construction worker	kārgar-e sāxtemāni	کارگر ساختمانی

project	porože	پروژه
architect	me'mār	معمار
worker	kārgar	کارگر

foundation (of a building)	šālude	شالوده
roof	bām	بام
foundation pile	pāye	پایه
wall	divār	دیوار

| reinforcing bars | milgerd | میلگرد |
| scaffolding | dārbast | داربست |

concrete	boton	بتن
granite	sang-e gerānit	سنگ گرانیت
stone	sang	سنگ
brick	ājor	آجر

sand	šen	شن
cement	simān	سیمان
plaster (for walls)	gač kāri	گچ کاری

to plaster (vt)	gačkār-i kardan	گچکاری کردن
paint	rang	رنگ
to paint (~ a wall)	rang kardan	رنگ کردن
barrel	boške	بشکه
crane	jarsaqil	جرثقیل
to lift, to hoist (vt)	boland kardan	بلند کردن
to lower (vt)	pāin āvardan	پائین آوردن
bulldozer	buldozer	بولدوزر
excavator	dastgāh-e haffāri	دستگاه حفاری
scoop, bucket	bil	بیل
to dig (excavate)	kandan	کندن
hard hat	kolāh-e imeni	کلاه ایمنی

Professions and occupations

104. Job search. Dismissal

job	kār	کار
staff (work force)	kārmandān	کارمندان
personnel	kādr	کادر

career	šoql	شغل
prospects (chances)	durnamā	دورنما
skills (mastery)	mahārat	مهارت

selection (screening)	entexāb	انتخاب
employment agency	āžāns-e kāryābi	آژانس کاریابی
résumé	rezume	رزومه
job interview	mosāhabe-ye kari	مصاحبه کاری
vacancy, opening	post-e xāli	پست خالی

salary, pay	hoquq	حقوق
fixed salary	darāmad-e s ābet	درآمد ثابت
pay, compensation	pardāxt	پرداخت

position (job)	šoql	شغل
duty (of employee)	vazife	وظیفه
range of duties	šarh-e vazāyef	شرح وظایف
busy (I'm ~)	mašqul	مشغول

| to fire (dismiss) | exrāj kardan | اخراج کردن |
| dismissal | exrāj | اخراج |

unemployment	bikāri	بیکاری
unemployed (n)	bikār	بیکار
retirement	mostamerri	مستمری
to retire (from job)	bāznešaste šodan	بازنشسته شدن

105. Business people

director	modir	مدیر
manager (director)	modir	مدیر
boss	ra'is	رئیس

superior	māfowq	مافوق
superiors	roasā	رؤسا
president	ra'is jomhur	رئیس جمهور

chairman	ra'is	رئیس
deputy (substitute)	mo'āven	معاون
assistant	mo'āven	معاون
secretary	monši	منشی
personal assistant	dastyār-e šaxsi	دستیار شخصی
businessman	bāzargān	بازرگان
entrepreneur	kārāfarin	کارآفرین
founder	moasses	مؤسس
to found (vt)	ta'sis kardan	تأسیس کردن
incorporator	hamkār	همکار
partner	šarik	شریک
stockholder	sahāmdār	سهامدار
millionaire	milyuner	میلیونر
billionaire	milyārder	میلیاردر
owner, proprietor	sāheb	صاحب
landowner	zamin-dār	زمین دار
client	xaridār	خریدار
regular client	xaridār-e dāemi	خریدار دائمی
buyer (customer)	xaridār	خریدار
visitor	bāzdid konande	بازدید کننده
professional (n)	herfe i	حرفه ای
expert	kāršenās	کارشناس
specialist	motexasses	متخصص
banker	kārmand-e bānk	کارمند بانک
broker	dallāl-e kārgozār	دلال کارگزار
cashier, teller	sanduqdār	صندوقدار
accountant	hesābdār	حسابدار
security guard	negahbān	نگهبان
investor	sarmāye gozār	سرمایه گذار
debtor	bedehkār	بدهکار
creditor	talabkār	طلبکار
borrower	vām girande	وام گیرنده
importer	vāred konande	وارد کننده
exporter	sāder konande	صادر کننده
manufacturer	towlid konande	تولید کننده
distributor	towzi' konande	توزیع کننده
middleman	vāsete	واسطه
consultant	mošāver	مشاور
sales representative	namāyande	نماینده
agent	namāyande	نماینده
insurance agent	namāyande-ye bime	نمایندۀ بیمه

106. Service professions

cook	āšpaz	آشپز
chef (kitchen chef)	sarāšpaz	سرآشپز
baker	nānvā	نانوا

bartender	motesaddi-ye bār	متصدی بار
waiter	pišxedmat	پیشخدمت
waitress	pišxedmat	پیشخدمت

lawyer, attorney	vakil	وکیل
lawyer (legal expert)	hoquq dān	حقوق دان
notary	daftardār	دفتردار

electrician	barq-e kār	برق کار
plumber	lule keš	لوله کش
carpenter	najjār	نجار

masseur	māsāž dahande	ماساژ دهنده
masseuse	māsāž dahande	ماساژ دهنده
doctor	pezešk	پزشک

taxi driver	rānande-ye tāksi	راننده تاکسی
driver	rānande	راننده
delivery man	peyk	پیک

chambermaid	mostaxdem	مستخدم
security guard	negahbān	نگهبان
flight attendant (fem.)	mehmāndār-e havāpeymā	مهماندار هواپیما

schoolteacher	mo'allem	معلم
librarian	ketābdār	کتابدار
translator	motarjem	مترجم
interpreter	motarjem-e šafāhi	مترجم شفاهی
guide	rāhnamā-ye tur	راهنمای تور

hairdresser	ārāyešgar	آرایشگر
mailman	nāme resān	نامه رسان
salesman (store staff)	forušande	فروشنده

gardener	bāqbān	باغبان
domestic servant	nowkar	نوکر
maid (female servant)	xedmatkār	خدمتکار
cleaner (cleaning lady)	zan-e nezāfatči	زن نظافتچی

107. Military professions and ranks

| private | sarbāz | سرباز |
| sergeant | goruhbān | گروهبان |

| lieutenant | sotvān | ستوان |
| captain | kāpitān | کاپیتان |

major	sargord	سرگرد
colonel	sarhang	سرهنگ
general	ženerāl	ژنرال
marshal	māršāl	مارشال
admiral	daryāsālār	دریاسالار

military (n)	nezāmi	نظامی
soldier	sarbāz	سرباز
officer	afsar	افسر
commander	farmāndeh	فرمانده

border guard	marzbān	مرزبان
radio operator	bisim či	بیسیم چی
scout (searcher)	ettelā'āti	اطلاعاتی
pioneer (sapper)	mohandes estehkāmāt	مهندس استحکامات
marksman	tirandāz	تیرانداز
navigator	nāvbar	ناور

108. Officials. Priests

| king | šāh | شاه |
| queen | maleke | ملکه |

| prince | šāhzāde | شاهزاده |
| princess | pranses | پرنسس |

| czar | tezār | تزار |
| czarina | maleke | ملکه |

president	ra'is jomhur	رئیس جمهور
Secretary (minister)	vazir	وزیر
prime minister	noxost vazir	نخست وزیر
senator	senātor	سناتور

diplomat	diplomāt	دیپلمات
consul	konsul	کنسول
ambassador	safir	سفیر
counsilor (diplomatic officer)	mošāver	مشاور

official, functionary (civil servant)	kārmand	کارمند
prefect	baxšdār	بخشدار
mayor	šahrdār	شهردار
judge	qāzi	قاضی
prosecutor (e.g., district attorney)	dādsetān	دادستان

missionary	misiyoner	میسیونر
monk	rāheb	راهب
abbot	rāheb-e bozorg	راهب بزرگ
rabbi	xāxām	خاخام

vizier	vazir	وزیر
shah	šāh	شاه
sheikh	šeyx	شیخ

109. Agricultural professions

beekeeper	zanburdār	زنبوردار
herder, shepherd	čupān	چوپان
agronomist	motexasses-e kešāvarzi	متخصص کشاورزی
cattle breeder	dāmparvar	دامپرور
veterinarian	dāmpezešk	دامپزشک

farmer	kešāvarz	کشاورز
winemaker	šarāb sāz	شراب ساز
zoologist	jānevar-šenās	جانور شناس
cowboy	gāvčerān	گاوچران

110. Art professions

| actor | bāzigar | بازیگر |
| actress | bāzigar | بازیگر |

| singer (masc.) | xānande | خواننده |
| singer (fem.) | xānande | خواننده |

| dancer (masc.) | raqqās | رقاص |
| dancer (fem.) | raqqāse | رقاصه |

| performer (masc.) | honarpiše | هنرپیشه |
| performer (fem.) | honarpiše | هنرپیشه |

musician	muzisiyan	موزیسین
pianist	piyānist	پیانیست
guitar player	gitārist	گیتاریست

conductor (orchestra ~)	rahbar-e orkestr	رهبر ارکستر
composer	āhangsāz	آهنگساز
impresario	modir-e operā	مدیر اپرا

film director	kārgardān	کارگردان
producer	tahiye konande	تهیه کننده
scriptwriter	senārist	سناریست
critic	montaqed	منتقد

writer	nevisande	نویسنده
poet	šā'er	شاعر
sculptor	mojassame sāz	مجسمه ساز
artist (painter)	naqqāš	نقاش

juggler	tardast	تردست
clown	dalqak	دلقک
acrobat	ākrobāt	آکروبات
magician	šo'bade bāz	شعبده باز

111. Various professions

doctor	pezešk	پزشک
nurse	parastār	پرستار
psychiatrist	ravānpezešk	روانپزشک
dentist	dandān pezešk	دندان پزشک
surgeon	jarrāh	جراح

astronaut	fazānavard	فضانورد
astronomer	setāre-šenās	ستاره شناس
pilot	xalabān	خلبان

driver (of taxi, etc.)	rānande	راننده
engineer (train driver)	rānande	راننده
mechanic	mekānik	مکانیک

miner	ma'danči	معدنچی
worker	kārgar	کارگر
locksmith	qofl sāz	قفل ساز
joiner (carpenter)	najjār	نجار
turner (lathe machine operator)	tarrāš kār	تراش کار
construction worker	kārgar-e sāxtemāni	کارگر ساختمانی
welder	juš kār	جوش کار

professor (title)	porofosor	پروفسور
architect	me'mār	معمار
historian	movarrex	مورخ
scientist	dānešmand	دانشمند
physicist	fizikdān	فیزیکدان
chemist (scientist)	šimi dān	شیمی دان

archeologist	bāstān-šenās	باستان شناس
geologist	zamin-šenās	زمین شناس
researcher (scientist)	pažuhešgar	پژوهشگر

babysitter	parastār bače	پرستار بچه
teacher, educator	āmuzgār	آموزگار
editor	virāstār	ویراستار
editor-in-chief	sardabir	سردبیر

| correspondent | xabarnegār | خبرنگار |
| typist (fem.) | māšin nevis | ماشین نویس |

designer	tarāh	طراح
computer expert	kāršenās kāmpiyuter	کارشناس کامپیوتر
programmer	barnāme-ye nevis	برنامه نویس
engineer (designer)	mohandes	مهندس

sailor	malavān	ملوان
seaman	malavān	ملوان
rescuer	nejāt-e dahande	نجات دهنده

fireman	ātaš nešān	آتش نشان
police officer	polis	پلیس
watchman	mohāfez	محافظ
detective	kārāgāh	کارآگاه

customs officer	ma'mur-e gomrok	مامور گمرک
bodyguard	mohāfez-e šaxsi	محافظ شخصی
prison guard	negahbān zendān	نگهبان زندان
inspector	bāzres	بازرس

sportsman	varzeškār	ورزشکار
trainer, coach	morabbi	مربی
butcher	qassāb	قصاب
cobbler (shoe repairer)	kaffāš	کفاش
merchant	bāzargān	بازرگان
loader (person)	bārbar	باربر

| fashion designer | tarrāh-e lebas | طراح لباس |
| model (fem.) | model-e zan | مدل زن |

112. Occupations. Social status

| schoolboy | dāneš-āmuz | دانش آموز |
| student (college ~) | dānešju | دانشجو |

philosopher	filsuf	فیلسوف
economist	eqtesāddān	اقتصاددان
inventor	moxtare'	مخترع

unemployed (n)	bikār	بیکار
retiree	bāznešaste	بازنشسته
spy, secret agent	jāsus	جاسوس

prisoner	zendāni	زندانی
striker	e'tesāb konande	اعتصاب کننده
bureaucrat	ma'mur-e edāri	مأمور اداری
traveler (globetrotter)	mosāfer	مسافر
gay, homosexual (n)	hamjens-e bāz	همجنس باز

hacker	haker	هکر
hippie	hipi	هیپی
bandit	rāhzan	راهزن
hit man, killer	ādamkoš	آدمکش
drug addict	mo'tād	معتاد
drug dealer	forušande-ye mavādd-e moxadder	فروشندۀ مواد مخدر
prostitute (fem.)	fāheše	فاحشه
pimp	jākeš	جاکش
sorcerer	jādugar	جادوگر
sorceress (evil ~)	jādugar	جادوگر
pirate	dozd-e daryāyi	دزد دریایی
slave	borde	برده
samurai	sāmurāyi	ساموراپی
savage (primitive)	vahši	وحشی

Sports

113. Kinds of sports. Sportspersons

sportsman	varzeškār	ورزشکار
kind of sports	anvā-e varzeš	انواع ورزش
basketball	basketbāl	بسکتبال
basketball player	basketbālist	بسکتبالیست
baseball	beysbāl	بیسبال
baseball player	beysbālist	بیسبالیست
soccer	futbāl	فوتبال
soccer player	futbālist	فوتبالیست
goalkeeper	darvāze bān	دروازه بان
hockey	hāki	هاکی
hockey player	hāki-ye bāz	هاکی باز
volleyball	vālibāl	والیبال
volleyball player	vālibālist	والیبالیست
boxing	boks	بوکس
boxer	boksor	بوکسور
wrestling	kešti	کشتی
wrestler	košti gir	کشتی گیر
karate	kārāte	کاراته
karate fighter	kārāte-e bāz	کاراته باز
judo	jodo	جودو
judo athlete	jodo bāz	جودو باز
tennis	tenis	تنیس
tennis player	tenis bāz	تنیس باز
swimming	šenā	شنا
swimmer	šenāgar	شناگر
fencing	šamširbāzi	شمشیربازی
fencer	šamširbāz	شمشیرباز
chess	šatranj	شطرنج
chess player	šatranj bāz	شطرنج باز

| alpinism | kuhnavardi | کوهنوردی |
| alpinist | kuhnavard | کوهنورد |

| running | do | دو |
| runner | davande | دونده |

| athletics | varzeš | ورزش |
| athlete | varzeškār | ورزشکار |

| horseback riding | asb savāri | اسب سواری |
| horse rider | savārkār | سوارکار |

figure skating	raqs ruy yax	رقص روی یخ
figure skater (masc.)	eskeyt bāz	اسکیت باز
figure skater (fem.)	eskeyt bāz	اسکیت باز

| powerlifting | vazne bardār-i | وزنه برداری |
| powerlifter | vazne bardār | وزنه بردار |

| car racing | mosābeqe-ye otomobilrāni | مسابقۀ اتومبیلرانی |
| racing driver | otomobilrān | اتومبیلران |

| cycling | dočarxe savāri | دوچرخه سواری |
| cyclist | dočarxe savār | دوچرخه سوار |

broad jump	pareš-e tul	پرش طول
pole vault	pareš bā neyze	پرش با نیزه
jumper	pareš konande	پرش کننده

114. Kinds of sports. Miscellaneous

football	futbāl-e āmrikāyi	فوتبال آمریکایی
badminton	badminton	بدمینتون
biathlon	biatlon	بیاتلون
billiards	bilyārd	بیلیارد

bobsled	surtme	سورتمه
bodybuilding	badansāzi	بدنسازی
water polo	vāterpolo	واترپولو
handball	handbāl	هندبال
golf	golf	گلف

rowing, crew	qāyeq rāni	قایق رانی
scuba diving	dāyving	دایوینگ
cross-country skiing	eski-ye sahrānavardi	اسکی صحرانوردی
table tennis (ping-pong)	ping pong	پینگ پونگ

sailing	qāyeq-rāni bādbani	قایق رانی بادبانی
rally racing	rāli	رالی
rugby	rāgbi	راگبی

| snowboarding | snowbord | اسنوبورد |
| archery | t randāzi bā kamān | تیراندازی با کمان |

115. Gym

| barbell | hālter | هالتر |
| dumbbells | dambel | دمبل |

training machine	māšin-e tamrin	ماشین تمرین
exercise bicycle	docarxe-ye tamrin	دوچرخه تمرین
treadmill	pist-e do	پیست دو

horizontal bar	bārfiks	بارفیکس
parallel bars	pārālel	پارالل
vault (vaulting horse)	xarak	خرک
mat (exercise ~)	tošak	تشک

jump rope	tanāb	طناب
aerobics	āirobik	ایروبیک
yoga	yugā	یوگا

116. Sports. Miscellaneous

Olympic Games	bāzihā-ye olampik	بازی‌های المپیک
winner	barande	برنده
to be winning	piruz šodan	پیروز شدن
to win (vi)	piruz šodan	پیروز شدن

| leader | rahbar | رهبر |
| to lead (vi) | lider budan | لیدر بودن |

first place	rotbe-ye avval	رتبه اول
second place	rotbe-ye dovvom	رتبه دوم
third place	rotbe-ye sevvom	رتبه سوم

medal	medāl	مدال
trophy	kāp	کاپ
prize cup (trophy)	jām	جام
prize (in game)	jāyeze	جایزه
main prize	jāyeze-ye asli	جایزهٔ اصلی

| record | rekord | رکورد |
| to set a record | rekord gozāštan | رکورد گذاشتن |

final	fināl	فینال
final (adj)	pāyāni	پایانی
champion	qahremān	قهرمان
championship	mεsābeqe-ye qahremāni	مسابقه قهرمانی

stadium	varzešgāh	ورزشگاه
stand (bleachers)	teribun	تریبون
fan, supporter	tarafdār	طرفدار
opponent, rival	raqib	رقیب
start (start line)	šoruʻ	شروع
finish line	entehā	انتها
defeat	šekast	شکست
to lose (not win)	bāxtan	باختن
referee	dāvar	داور
jury (judges)	heyʻat-e dāvarān	هیئت داوران
score	emtiyāz	امتیاز
tie	mosāvi	مساوی
to tie (vi)	bāzi rā mosāvi kardan	بازی رامساوی کردن
point	emtiyāz	امتیاز
result (final score)	natije	نتیجه
period	dowre	دوره
half-time	hāf tāym	هاف تایم
doping	doping	دوپینگ
to penalize (vt)	jarime kardan	جریمه کردن
to disqualify (vt)	rad-e salāhiyat kardan	رد صلاحیت کردن
apparatus	asbāb	اسباب
javelin	neyze	نیزه
shot (metal ball)	vazne	وزنه
ball (snooker, etc.)	tup	توپ
aim (target)	hadaf	هدف
target	nešangah	نشانگاه
to shoot (vi)	tirandāzi kardan	تیراندازی کردن
accurate (~ shot)	dorost	درست
trainer, coach	morabbi	مربی
to train (sb)	tamrin dādan	تمرین دادن
to train (vi)	tamrin kardan	تمرین کردن
training	tamrin	تمرین
gym	sālon-e varzeš	سالن ورزش
exercise (physical)	tamrin	تمرین
warm-up (athlete ~)	garm kardan	گرم کردن

Education

117. School

school	madrese	مدرسه
principal (headmaster)	modir-e madrese	مدیر مدرسه
pupil (boy)	dāneš-āmuz	دانش آموز
pupil (girl)	dāneš-āmuz	دانش آموز
schoolboy	dāneš-āmuz	دانش آموز
schoolgirl	dāneš-āmuz	دانش آموز
to teach (sb)	āmuxtan	آموختن
to learn (language, etc.)	yād gereftan	یاد گرفتن
to learn by heart	az hefz kardan	از حفظ کردن
to learn (~ to count, etc.)	yād gereftan	یاد گرفتن
to be in school	tahsil kardan	تحصیل کردن
to go to school	madrese raftan	مدرسه رفتن
alphabet	alefbā	الفبا
subject (at school)	mabhas	مبحث
classroom	kelās	کلاس
lesson	dars	درس
recess	zang-e tafrih	زنگ تفریح
school bell	zang	زنگ
school desk	miz-e tahrir	میز تحریر
chalkboard	taxte-ye siyāh	تخته سیاه
grade	nomre	نمره
good grade	nomre-ye xub	نمرهٔ خوب
bad grade	nomre-ye bad	نمرهٔ بد
to give a grade	nomre gozāštan	نمره گذاشتن
mistake, error	eštebāh	اشتباه
to make mistakes	eštebāh kardan	اشتباه کردن
to correct (an error)	eslāh kardan	اصلاح کردن
cheat sheet	taqallob	تقلب
homework	taklif manzel	تکلیف منزل
exercise (in education)	tamrin	تمرین
to be present	hozur dāštan	حضور داشتن
to be absent	qāyeb budan	غایب بودن
to miss school	az madrese qāyeb budan	ازمدرسه غایب بودن

to punish (vt)	tanbih kardan	تنبیه کردن
punishment	tanbih	تنبیه
conduct (behavior)	raftār	رفتار

report card	gozāreš-e ruzāne	گزارش روزانه
pencil	medād	مداد
eraser	pāk kon	پاک کن
chalk	gač	گچ
pencil case	qalamdān	قلمدان

schoolbag	kif madrese	کیف مدرسه
pen	xodkār	خودکار
school notebook	daftar	دفتر
textbook	ketāb-e darsi	کتاب درسی
compasses	pargār	پرگار

| to make technical drawings | rasm kardan | رسم کردن |
| technical drawing | rasm-e fani | رسم فنی |

poem	še'r	شعر
by heart (adv)	az hefz	از حفظ
to learn by heart	az hefz kardan	از حفظ کردن

school vacation	ta'tilāt	تعطیلات
to be on vacation	dar ta'tilāt budan	در تعطیلات بودن
to spend one's vacation	ta'tilāt rā gozarāndan	تعطیلات را گذراندن

test (written math ~)	emtehān	امتحان
essay (composition)	enšā'	انشاء
dictation	dikte	دیکته
exam (examination)	emtehān	امتحان
to take an exam	emtehān dādan	امتحان دادن
experiment (e.g., chemistry ~)	āzmāyeš	آزمایش

118. College. University

academy	farhangestān	فرهنگستان
university	dānešgāh	دانشگاه
faculty (e.g., ~ of Medicine)	dāneškade	دانشکده

student (masc.)	dānešju	دانشجو
student (fem.)	dānešju	دانشجو
lecturer (teacher)	ostād	استاد

lecture hall, room	kelās	کلاس
graduate	fāreqottahsil	فارغ التحصیل
diploma	diplom	دیپلم

dissertation	pāyān nāme	پایان نامه
study (report)	tahqiqe elmi	تحقیق علمی
laboratory	āzmāyešgāh	آزمایشگاه

lecture	soxanrāni	سخنرانی
coursemate	ha mdowre i	هم دوره ای
scholarship	burse tahsili	بورس تحصیلی
academic degree	daraje-ye elmi	درجهٔ علمی

119. Sciences. Disciplines

mathematics	riyāziyāt	ریاضیات
algebra	jabr	جبر
geometry	hendese	هندسه

astronomy	setāre-šenāsi	ستاره شناسی
biology	zist-šenāsi	زیست شناسی
geography	joqrāfiyā	جغرافیا
geology	zamin-šenāsi	زمین شناسی
history	tārix	تاریخ

medicine	pezeški	پزشکی
pedagogy	olume tarbiyati	علوم تربیتی
law	hoquq	حقوق

physics	fizik	فیزیک
chemistry	šimi	شیمی
philosophy	falsafe	فلسفه
psychology	ravānšenāsi	روانشناسی

120. Writing system. Orthography

grammar	gerāmer	گرامر
vocabulary	vājegān	واژگان
phonetics	sadā-šenāsi	صداشناسی

noun	esm	اسم
adjective	sefat	صفت
verb	fe'l	فعل
adverb	qeyd	قید

pronoun	zamir	ضمیر
interjection	harf-e nedā	حرف ندا
preposition	harf-e ezāfe	حرف اضافه

root	riše-ye kalame	ریشه کلمه
ending	pasvand	پسوند
prefix	pišvand	پیشوند

syllable	hejā	هجا
suffix	pasvand	پسوند
stress mark	fešar-e hejā	فشار هجا
apostrophe	āpostrof	آپوستروف
period, dot	noqte	نقطه
comma	virgul	ویرگول
semicolon	noqte virgul	نقطه ویرگول
colon	donoqte	دونقطه
ellipsis	čand noqte	چند نقطه
question mark	alāmat-e soāl	علامت سؤال
exclamation point	alāmat-e taajjob	علامت تعجب
quotation marks	giyume	گیومه
in quotation marks	dar giyume	در گیومه
parenthesis	parāntez	پرانتز
in parenthesis	dar parāntez	در پرانتز
hyphen	xatt-e vāsel	خط واصل
dash	xatt-e tire	خط تیره
space (between words)	fāsele	فاصله
letter	harf	حرف
capital letter	harf-e bozorg	حرف بزرگ
vowel (n)	sedādār	صدادار
consonant (n)	sāmet	صامت
sentence	jomle	جمله
subject	nahād	نهاد
predicate	gozāre	گزاره
line	satr	سطر
on a new line	sar-e satr	سر سطر
paragraph	band	بند
word	kalame	کلمه
group of words	ebārat	عبارت
expression	bayān	بیان
synonym	moterādef	مترادف
antonym	motezād	متضاد
rule	qā'ede	قاعده
exception	estesnā	استثنا
correct (adj)	sahih	صحیح
conjugation	sarf	صرف
declension	sarf-e kalemāt	صرف کلمات
nominal case	hālat	حالت
question	soāl	سؤال

| to underline (vt) | xatt kešidan | خط کشیدن |
| dotted line | noqte čin | نقطه چین |

121. Foreign languages

language	zabān	زبان
foreign (adj)	xāreji	خارجی
foreign language	zabān-e xāreji	زبان خارجی
to study (vt)	dars xāndan	درس خواندن
to learn (language, etc.)	yād gereftan	یاد گرفتن

to read (vi, vt)	xāndan	خواندن
to speak (vi, vt)	harf zadan	حرف زدن
to understand (vt)	fahmidan	فهمیدن
to write (vt)	neveštan	نوشتن

fast (adv)	sari'	سریع
slowly (adv)	āheste	آهسته
fluently (adv)	ravān	روان

rules	qavā'ed	قواعد
grammar	gerāmer	گرامر
vocabulary	vājegān	واژگان
phonetics	āvā-šenāsi	آواشناسی

textbook	ketāb-e darsi	کتاب درسی
dictionary	farhang-e loqat	فرهنگ لغت
teach-yourself book	xod-āmuz	خودآموز
phrasebook	ketāb-e mokāleme	کتاب مکالمه

cassette, tape	kāst	کاست
videotape	kāst-e video	کاست ویدئو
CD, compact disc	si-di	سیدی
DVD	dey vey dey	دی وی دی

alphabet	alefbā	الفبا
to spell (vt)	heji kardan	هجی کردن
pronunciation	talaffoz	تلفظ

accent	lahje	لهجه
with an accent	bā lahje	با لهجه
without an accent	bi lahje	بی لهجه

| word | kalame | کلمه |
| meaning | ma'ni | معنی |

course (e.g., a French ~)	dowre	دوره
to sign up	nām-nevisi kardan	نام نویسی کردن
teacher	ostād	استاد
translation (process)	tarjome	ترجمه

translation (text, etc.)	tarjome	ترجمه
translator	motarjem	مترجم
interpreter	motarjem-e šafāhi	مترجم شفاهی

| polyglot | čand zabāni | چند زبانی |
| memory | hāfeze | حافظه |

122. Fairy tale characters

Santa Claus	bābā noel	بابا نوئل
Cinderella	sinderelā	سیندرلا
mermaid	pari-ye daryāyi	پری دریایی
Neptune	nepton	نپتون

magician, wizard	sāher	ساحر
fairy	sāher	ساحر
magic (adj)	jāduyi	جادویی
magic wand	asā-ye sehrāmiz	عصای سحرآمیز

fairy tale	afsāne	افسانه
miracle	mo'jeze	معجزه
dwarf	kutule	کوتوله
to turn into ...	tabdil šodan	تبدیل شدن

ghost	šabah	شبح
phantom	šabah	شبح
monster	qul	غول
dragon	eždehā	اژدها
giant	qul	غول

123. Zodiac Signs

Aries	borj-e haml	برج حمل
Taurus	borj-e sowr	برج ثور
Gemini	borj-e jowzā	برج جوزا
Cancer	saratān	سرطان
Leo	šir	شیر
Virgo	borj-e sonbole	برج سنبله

Libra	borj-e mizān	برج میزان
Scorpio	borj-e aqrab	برج عقرب
Sagittarius	borj-e qows	برج قوس
Capricorn	borj-e jeddi	برج جدی
Aquarius	borj-e dalow	برج دلو
Pisces	borj-e hut	برج حوت

| character | šaxsiyat | شخصیت |
| character traits | xosusiyāt-e axlāqi | خصوصیات اخلاقی |

behavior	raftār	رفتار
to tell fortunes	fāl gereftan	فال گرفتن
fortune-teller	fālgir	فالگیر
horoscope	tāle' bini	طالع بینی

Arts

124. Theater

theater	teātr	تئاتر
opera	operā	اپرا
operetta	operā-ye kučak	اپرای کوچک
ballet	bāle	باله
theater poster	e'lān-e namāyeš	اعلان نمایش
troupe (theatrical company)	hey'at honarpišegān	هیئت هنرپیشگان
tour	safar	سفر
to be on tour	dar tur budan	در تور بودن
to rehearse (vi, vt)	tamrin kardan	تمرین کردن
rehearsal	tamrin	تمرین
repertoire	roperator	رپراتور
performance	namāyeš	نمایش
theatrical show	namāyeš	نمایش
play	namāyeš nāme	نمایش نامه
ticket	belit	بلیط
box office (ticket booth)	belit-foruši	بلیت فروشی
lobby, foyer	lābi	لابی
coat check (cloakroom)	komod-e lebās	کمد لباس
coat check tag	žeton	ژتون
binoculars	durbin	دوربین
usher	rāhnamā	راهنما
orchestra seats	sandali-ye orkestr	صندلی ارکستر
balcony	bālkon	بالکن
dress circle	bālkon-e avval	بالکن اول
box	jāygāh-e vižhe	جایگاه ویژه
row	radif	ردیف
seat	jā	جا
audience	hozzār	حضار
spectator	tamāšāči	تماشاچی
to clap (vi, vt)	kaf zadan	کف زدن
applause	tašviq	تشویق
ovation	šādi-va sorur	شادی و سرور
stage	sahne	صحنه
curtain	parde	پرده
scenery	sahne	صحنه

backstage	pošt-e sahne	پشت صحنه
scene (e.g., the last ~)	sahne	صحنه
act	parde	پرده
intermission	ānterākt	آنتراکت

125. Cinema

| actor | bāzigar | بازیگر |
| actress | bāzigar | بازیگر |

movies (industry)	sinamā	سینما
movie	film	فیلم
episode	qesmat	قسمت

detective movie	film-e polisi	فیلم پلیسی
action movie	film-e akšen	فیلم اکشن
adventure movie	film-e mājarāyi	فیلم ماجرایی
science fiction movie	film-e elmi-ye taxayyoli	فیلم علمی تخیلی
horror movie	film-e tarsnāk	فیلم ترسناک

comedy movie	komedi	کمدی
melodrama	meloderām	ملودرام
drama	derām	درام

fictional movie	film-e honari	فیلم هنری
documentary	film-e mostanad	فیلم مستند
cartoon	kārton	کارتون
silent movies	film-e sāmet	فیلم صامت

role (part)	naqš	نقش
leading role	naqš-e asli	نقش اصلی
to play (vi, vt)	bāzi kardan	بازی کردن

movie star	setāre-ye sinamā	ستارۀ سینما
well-known (adj)	mašhur	مشهور
famous (adj)	mašhur	مشهور
popular (adj)	saršenās	سرشناس

script (screenplay)	senāriyo	سناریو
scriptwriter	senārist	سناریست
movie director	kārgardān	کارگردان
producer	tahiye konande	تهیه کننده
assistant	dastyār	دستیار
cameraman	filmbardār	فیلمبردار
stuntman	badalkār	بدلکار
double (stuntman)	dublur	دوبلور

to shoot a movie	film gereftan	فیلم گرفتن
audition, screen test	test	تست
shooting	film bardār-i	فیلم برداری

movie crew	goruh film bar dār-i	گروه فیلم برداری
movie set	mahal film bar dār-i	محل فیلم برداری
camera	durbin	دوربین

movie theater	sinamā	سینما
screen (e.g., big ~)	parde	پرده
to show a movie	film-e nešān dādan	فیلم نشان دادن

soundtrack	musiqi-ye matn	موسیقی متن
special effects	jelvehā-ye vižhe	جلوه های ویژه
subtitles	zirnevis	زیرنویس
credits	titrāj	تیتراژ
translation	tarjome	ترجمه

126. Painting

art	honar	هنر
fine arts	honarhā-ye zibā	هنرهای زیبا
art gallery	gāleri-ye honari	گالری هنری
art exhibition	namāyešgāh-e honari	نمایشگاه هنری

painting (art)	naqqāši	نقاشی
graphic art	honar-e gerāfik	هنر گرافیک
abstract art	honar-e ābestre	هنر آبستره
impressionism	ampersiyonism	امپرسیونیسم

picture (painting)	tasvir	تصویر
drawing	naqqāši	نقاشی
poster	poster	پوستر

illustration (picture)	tasvir	تصویر
miniature	minyātor	مینیاتور
copy (of painting, etc.)	nosxe	نسخه
reproduction	taksir	تکثیر

mosaic	muzāik	موزائیک
stained glass window	naqqāši ruy šiše	نقاشی روی شیشه
fresco	naqqāši ruy gač	نقاشی روی گچ
engraving	gerāvur	گراور

bust (sculpture)	mojassame-ye nimtane	مجسمهٔ نیم تنه
sculpture	mojassame sāz-i	مجسمه سازی
statue	mojassame	مجسمه
plaster of Paris	gač	گچ
plaster (as adj)	gači	گچی

portrait	temsāl	تمثال
self-portrait	tasvir-e naqqāš	تصویر نقاش
landscape painting	manzare	منظره
still life	tabi'at-e bijān	طبیعت بیجان

| caricature | kārikātor | کاریکاتور |
| sketch | tarh-e moqaddamāti | طرح مقدماتی |

paint	rang	رنگ
watercolor paint	āb-o rang	آب ورنگ
oil (paint)	rowqan	روغن
pencil	medād	مداد
India ink	morakkab	مرکب
charcoal	zoqāl	زغال

| to draw (vi, vt) | naqqāši kardan | نقاشی کردن |
| to paint (vi, vt) | naqqāši kardan | نقاشی کردن |

to pose (vi)	žest gereftan	ژست گرفتن
artist's model (masc.)	model-e naqqāši	مدل نقاشی
artist's model (fem.)	model-e naqqāši	مدل نقاشی

artist (painter)	naqqāš	نقاش
work of art	asar-e honari	اثر هنری
masterpiece	šāhkār	شاهکار
studio (artist's workroom)	kārgāh	کارگاه

canvas (cloth)	bum-e naqāši	بوم نقاشی
easel	sepāye-ye naqqāši	سه پایهٔ نقاشی
palette	taxte-ye rang	تختهٔ رنگ

frame (picture ~, etc.)	qāb	قاب
restoration	maremmat	مرمت
to restore (vt)	marammat kardan	مرمت کردن

127. Literature & Poetry

literature	adabiyāt	ادبیات
author (writer)	moallef	مؤلف
pseudonym	taxallos	تخلص

book	ketāb	کتاب
volume	jeld	جلد
table of contents	fehrest	فهرست
page	safhe	صفحه
main character	qahremān-e asli	قهرمان اصلی
autograph	dast-e xat	دست خط

short story	hekāyat	حکایت
story (novella)	dāstān	داستان
novel	ramān	رمان
work (writing)	ta'lif	تألیف
fable	afsāne	افسانه
detective novel	dastane jenai	داستان جنایی
poem (verse)	še'r	شعر

poetry	še'r	شعر
poem (epic, ballad)	še'r	شعر
poet	šā'er	شاعر
fiction	dāstān	داستان
science fiction	elmi-ye taxayyoli	علمی تخیلی
adventures	sargozašt	سرگذشت
educational literature	adabiyāt-e āmuzeši	ادبیات آموزشی
children's literature	adabiyāt-e kudak	ادبیات کودک

128. Circus

circus	sirak	سیرک
traveling circus	sirak-e sayār	سیرک سیار
program	barnāme	برنامه
performance	namāyeš	نمایش
act (circus ~)	parde	پرده
circus ring	sahne-ye sirak	صحنه سیرک
pantomime (act)	pāntomim	پانتومیم
clown	dalqak	دلقک
acrobat	ākrobāt	آکروبات
acrobatics	band-e bāzi	بند بازی
gymnast	žimināstik kār	ژیمناستیک کار
gymnastics	žimināstik	ژیمناستیک
somersault	salto	سالتو
athlete (strongman)	qavi heykal	قوی هیکل
tamer (e.g., lion ~)	rām konande	رام کننده
rider (circus horse ~)	savārkār	سوارکار
assistant	dastyār	دستیار
stunt	širin kāri	شیرین کاری
magic trick	šo'bade bāzi	شعبده بازی
conjurer, magician	šo'bade bāz	شعبده باز
juggler	tardast	تردست
to juggle (vi, vt)	tardasti kardan	تردستی کردن
animal trainer	morabbi-ye heyvānāt	مربی حیوانات
animal training	ta'lim heyvānāt	تعلیم حیوانات
to train (animals)	tarbiyat kardan	تربیت کردن

129. Music. Pop music

music	musiqi	موسیقی
musician	muzisiyan	موزیسین

musical instrument	abzār-e musiqi	ابزار موسیقی
to play …	navāxtan	نواختن
guitar	gitār	گیتار
violin	viyolon	ویولون
cello	viyolonsel	ویولون سل
double bass	konterbās	کونترباس
harp	čang	چنگ
piano	piyāno	پیانو
grand piano	piyāno-e bozorg	پیانوی بزرگ
organ	arg	ارگ
wind instruments	sāzhā-ye bādi	سازهای بادی
oboe	abva	ابوا
saxophone	saksofon	ساکسوفون
clarinet	qare ney	قره نی
flute	folut	فلوت
trumpet	šeypur	شیپور
accordion	ākordeon	آکوردئون
drum	tabl	طبل
duo	caste-ye do nafare	دستهٔ دو نفره
trio	caste-ye se nafar-i	دستهٔ سه نفری
quartet	daste-ye čāhārnafari	دستهٔ چهارنفری
choir	kar	کر
orchestra	orkesr	ارکستر
pop music	musiqi-ye pāp	موسیقی پاپ
rock music	musiqi-ye rāk	موسیقی راک
rock group	goruh-e rāk	گروه راک
jazz	jāz	جاز
idol	mahbub	محبوب
admirer, fan	havādār	هوادار
concert	konsert	کنسرت
symphony	samfoni	سمفونی
composition	tasnif	تصنیف
to compose (write)	tasnif kardan	تصنیف کردن
singing (n)	āvāz	آواز
song	tarāne	ترانه
tune (melody)	āhang	آهنگ
rhythm	ritm	ریتم
blues	musiqi-ye boluz	موسیقی بلوز
sheet music	daftar-e not	دفتر نت
baton	čub-e rahbari	چوب رهبری
bow	ārše	آرشه
string	sim	سیم
case (e.g., guitar ~)	qalāf	غلاف

Rest. Entertainment. Travel

130. Trip. Travel

tourism, travel	gardešgari	گردشگری
tourist	turist	توریست
trip, voyage	mosāferat	مسافرت
adventure	mājarā	ماجرا
trip, journey	safar	سفر
vacation	moraxxasi	مرخصی
to be on vacation	dar moraxassi budan	در مرخصی بودن
rest	esterāhat	استراحت
train	qatār	قطار
by train	bā qatār	با قطار
airplane	havāpeymā	هواپیما
by airplane	bā havāpeymā	با هواپیما
by car	bā otomobil	با اتومبیل
by ship	dar kešti	با کشتی
luggage	bār	بار
suitcase	čamedān	چمدان
luggage cart	čarx-e hamle bar	چرخ حمل بار
passport	gozarnāme	گذرنامه
visa	ravādid	روادید
ticket	belit	بلیط
air ticket	belit-e havāpeymā	بلیط هواپیما
guidebook	ketāb-e rāhnamā	کتاب راهنما
map (tourist ~)	naqše	نقشه
area (rural ~)	mahal	محل
place, site	jā	جا
exotica (n)	qarāyeb	غرایب
exotic (adj)	qarib	غریب
amazing (adj)	heyrat angiz	حیرت انگیز
group	goruh	گروه
excursion, sightseeing tour	gardeš	گردش
guide (person)	rāhnamā-ye tur	راهنمای تور

131. Hotel

hotel	hotel	هتل
motel	motel	متل
three-star (~ hotel)	se setāre	سه ستاره
five-star	panj setāre	پنج ستاره
to stay (in a hotel, etc.)	māndan	ماندن
room	otāq	اتاق
single room	ɔtāq-e yeknafare	اتاق یک نفره
double room	ɔtāq-e do nafare	اتاق دو نفره
to book a room	ɔtāq rezerv kardan	اتاق رزرو کردن
half board	nim pānsiyon	نیم پانسیون
full board	pānsiyon	پانسیون
with bath	bā vān	با وان
with shower	bā duš	با دوش
satellite television	televiziyon-e māhvārei	تلویزیون ماهواره ای
air-conditioner	tahviye-ye matbu'	تهویه مطبوع
towel	howle	حوله
key	kelid	کلید
administrator	edāre-ye konande	اداره کننده
chambermaid	mostaxdem	مستخدم
porter, bellboy	bārbar	باربر
doorman	darbān	دربان
restaurant	resturān	رستوران
pub, bar	bār	بار
breakfast	sobhāne	صبحانه
dinner	šām	شام
buffet	bufe	بوفه
lobby	lābi	لابی
elevator	āsānsor	آسانسور
DO NOT DISTURB	mozāhem našavid	مزاحم نشوید
NO SMOKING	sigār kešidan mamnu'	سیگار کشیدن ممنوع

132. Books. Reading

book	ketāb	کتاب
author	moallef	مؤلف
writer	nevisande	نویسنده
to write (~ a book)	neveštan	نوشتن
reader	xānande	خواننده
to read (vi, vt)	xāndan	خواندن

reading (activity)	motāle'e	مطالعه
silently (to oneself)	be ārāmi	به آرامی
aloud (adv)	boland	بلند
to publish (vt)	montašer kardan	منتشر کردن
publishing (process)	entešār	انتشار
publisher	nāšer	ناشر
publishing house	entešārāt	انتشارات
to come out (be released)	montašer šodan	منتشر شدن
release (of a book)	našr	نشر
print run	tirāž	تیراژ
bookstore	ketāb-foruši	کتاب فروشی
library	ketābxāne	کتابخانه
story (novella)	dāstān	داستان
short story	hekāyat	حکایت
novel	ramān	رمان
detective novel	dastane jenai	داستان جنایی
memoirs	xāterāt	خاطرات
legend	afsāne	افسانه
myth	osture	اسطوره
poetry, poems	še'r	شعر
autobiography	zendegināme	زندگینامه
selected works	āsār-e montaxab	آثار منتخب
science fiction	elmi-ye taxayyoli	علمی تخیلی
title	onvān	عنوان
introduction	moqaddame	مقدمه
title page	safhe-ye onvān	صفحه عنوان
chapter	fasl	فصل
extract	gozide	گزیده
episode	qesmat	قسمت
plot (storyline)	suže	سوژه
contents	mazmun	مضمون
table of contents	fehrest	فهرست
main character	qahremān-e asli	قهرمان اصلی
volume	jeld	جلد
cover	jeld	جلد
binding	sahhāfi	صحافی
bookmark	čub-e alef	چوب الف
page	safhe	صفحه
to page through	varaq zadan	ورق زدن
margins	hāšiye	حاشیه
annotation (marginal note, etc.)	hāšiye nevisi	حاشیه نویسی

footnote	pāvaraqi	پاورقی
text	matn	متن
type, font	font	فونت
misprint, typo	qalat čāpi	غلط چاپی
translation	tarjome	ترجمه
to translate (vt)	tarjome kardan	ترجمه کردن
original (n)	nosxe-ye asli	نسخهٔ اصلی
famous (adj)	mašhur	مشهور
unknown (not famous)	nāšenāxte	ناشناخته
interesting (adj)	jāleb	جالب
bestseller	por foruš	پر فروش
dictionary	farhang-e loqat	فرهنگ لغت
textbook	ketāb-e darsi	کتاب درسی
encyclopedia	dāyeratolma'āref	دایره المعارف

133. Hunting. Fishing

hunting	šekār	شکار
to hunt (vi, vt)	šekār kardan	شکار کردن
hunter	šekārči	شکارچی
to shoot (vi)	tirandāzi kardan	تیراندازی کردن
rifle	tofang	تفنگ
bullet (shell)	fešang	فشنگ
shot (lead balls)	sāčme	ساچمه
steel trap	tale	تله
snare (for birds, etc.)	dām	دام
to fall into the steel trap	dar tale oftādan	در تله افتادن
to lay a steel trap	tale gozāštan	تله گذاشتن
poacher	šekārči-ye qeyr-e qānuni	شکارچی غیر قانونی
game (in hunting)	šekār	شکار
hound dog	sag-e šekāri	سگ شکاری
safari	safar-e ektešāfi āfriqā	سفر اکتشافی آفریقا
mounted animal	heyvān-e model	حیوان مدل
fisherman, angler	māhigir	ماهیگیر
fishing (angling)	māhigiri	ماهیگیری
to fish (vi)	māhi gereftan	ماهی گرفتن
fishing rod	čub māhi gir-i	چوب ماهی گیری
fishing line	nax-e māhigiri	نخ ماهیگیری
hook	qollāb	قلاب
float, bobber	šenāvar	شناور
bait	to'me	طعمه
to cast a line	qollāb andāxtan	قلاب انداختن

to bite (ab. fish)	gāz gereftan	گاز گرفتن
catch (of fish)	seyd	صید
ice-hole	surāx dar yax	سوراخ دریخ
fishing net	tur	تور
boat	qāyeq	قایق
to net (to fish with a net)	bā tur-e māhi gereftan	با تورماهی گرفتن
to cast[throw] the net	tur andāxtan	تور انداختن
to haul the net in	tur rā birun āvardan	تور را بیرون آوردن
to fall into the net	be tur oftādan	به تور افتادن
whaler (person)	seyād-e nahang	صیاد نهنگ
whaleboat	kešti-ye seyd-e nahang	کشتی صید نهنگ
harpoon	neyze	نیزه

134. Games. Billiards

billiards	bilyārd	بیلیارد
billiard room, hall	otāq-e bilyārd	اتاق بیلیارد
ball (snooker, etc.)	tup	توپ
to pocket a ball	tup vāred-e pākat kardan	توپ وارد پاکت کردن
cue	čub-e bilyārd	چوب بیلیارد
pocket	pākat	پاکت

135. Games. Playing cards

diamonds	xešt	خشت
spades	peyk	پیک
hearts	del	دل
clubs	xāj	خاج
ace	tak xāl	تک خال
king	šāh	شاه
queen	bi bi	بی بی
jack, knave	sarbāz	سرباز
playing card	varaq	ورق
cards	varaq	ورق
trump	xāl-e hokm	خال حکم
deck of cards	daste-ye varaq	دستۀ ورق
point	xāl	خال
to deal (vi, vt)	varaq dādan	ورق دادن
to shuffle (cards)	bar zadan	بر زدن
lead, turn (n)	harekat	حرکت
cardsharp	moteqalleb	متقلب

136. Rest. Games. Miscellaneous

to stroll (vi, vt)	gardeš kardan	گردش کردن
stroll (leisurely walk)	gardeš	گردش
car ride	siyāhat	سیاحت
adventure	mājarā	ماجرا
picnic	pik nik	پیک نیک
game (chess, etc.)	bāzi	بازی
player	bāzikon	بازیکن
game (one ~ of chess)	dor-e bazi	دوربازی
collector (e.g., philatelist)	kolleksiyoner	کلکسیونر
to collect (stamps, etc.)	am'-e āvari kardan	جمع آوری کردن
collection	koleksiyon	کلکسیون
crossword puzzle	kalamāt-e moteqāte'	کلمات متقاطع
racetrack	meydān-e asb-e davāni	میدان اسب دوانی
(horse racing venue)		
disco (discotheque)	disko	دیسکو
sauna	sonā	سونا
lottery	baxt-e āzmāyi	بخت آزمایی
camping trip	rāh peymāyi	راه پیمایی
camp	ordugāh	اردوگاه
tent (for camping)	čādor	چادر
compass	qotb namā	قطب نما
camper	kamp nešin	کمپ نشین
to watch (movie, etc.)	tamāšā kardan	تماشا کردن
viewer	tamāšāči	تماشاچی
TV show (TV program)	barnāme-ye televiziyoni	برنامه تلویزیونی

137. Photography

camera (photo)	durbin-e akkāsi	دوربین عکاسی
photo, picture	aks	عکس
photographer	akkās	عکاس
photo studio	ātolye-ye akkāsi	آتلیۀ عکاسی
photo album	ālbom-e aks	آلبوم عکس
camera lens	lenz-e durbin	لنز دوربین
telephoto lens	lenz-e tale-ye foto	لنز تله فوتو
filter	filter	فیلتر
lens	lenz	لنز
optics (high-quality ~)	optik	اپتیک
diaphragm (aperture)	diyāfrāgm	دیافراگم

exposure time (shutter speed)	sor'at-e bāz šodan-e lenz	سرعت بازشدن لنز
viewfinder	namā yāb	نما یاب
digital camera	durbin-e dijitāl	دوربین دیجیتال
tripod	se pāye	سه پایه
flash	feleš	فلش
to photograph (vt)	akkāsi kardan	عکاسی کردن
to take pictures	aks gereftan	عکس گرفتن
to have one's picture taken	aks gereftan	عکس گرفتن
focus	noqte-ye kānuni	نقطه کانونی
to focus	motemarkez kardan	متمرکز کردن
sharp, in focus (adj)	vāzeh	واضح
sharpness	vozuh	وضوح
contrast	konterāst	کنتراست
contrast (as adj)	konterāst	کنتراست
picture (photo)	aks	عکس
negative (n)	film-e negātiv	فیلم نگاتیو
film (a roll of ~)	film	فیلم
frame (still)	čārcub	چارچوب
to print (photos)	čāp kardan	چاپ کردن

138. Beach. Swimming

beach	pelāž	پلاژ
sand	šen	شن
deserted (beach)	xāli	خالی
suntan	hammām-e āftāb	حمام آفتاب
to get a tan	hammām-e āftāb gereftan	حمام آفتاب گرفتن
tan (adj)	boronze	برنزه
sunscreen	kerem-e zedd-e āftāb	کرم ضد آفتاب
bikini	māyo-ye do tekke	مایوی دو تکه
bathing suit	māyo	مایو
swim trunks	māyo	مایو
swimming pool	estaxr	استخر
to swim (vi)	šenā kardan	شنا کردن
shower	duš	دوش
to change (one's clothes)	lebās avaz kardan	لباس عوض کردن
towel	howle	حوله
boat	qāyeq	قایق
motorboat	qāyeq-e motori	قایق موتوری
water ski	eski-ye ruy-ye āb	اسکی روی آب

paddle boat	qāyeq-e pedāli	قایق پدالی
surfing	mowj savāri	موج سواری
surfer	mowj savār	موج سوار
scuba set	eskowba	اسکوبا
flippers (swim fins)	bālehā-ye qavvāsi	باله های غواصی
mask (diving ~)	māsk	ماسک
diver	qavvās	غواص
to dive (vi)	širje raftan	شیرجه رفتن
underwater (adv)	zir-e ābi	زیر آبی
beach umbrella	čatr	چتر
sunbed (lounger)	sandali-ye rāhati	صندلی راحتی
sunglasses	eynak āftābi	عینک آفتابی
air mattress	tošak-e ābi	تشک آبی
to play (amuse oneself)	bāzi kardan	بازی کردن
to go for a swim	ābtani kardan	آبتنی کردن
beach ball	tup	توپ
to inflate (vt)	bād kardan	باد کردن
inflatable, air (adj)	bādi	بادی
wave	mowj	موج
buoy (line of ~s)	šenāvar	شناور
to drown (ab. person)	qarq šodan	غرق شدن
to save, to rescue	najāt dādan	نجات دادن
life vest	jeliqe-ye nejāt	جلیقۀ نجات
to observe, to watch	mošāhede kardan	مشاهده کردن
lifeguard	nejāt-e dahande	نجات دهنده

TECHNICAL EQUIPMENT. TRANSPORTATION

Technical equipment

139. Computer

computer	kāmpiyuter	کامپیوتر
notebook, laptop	lap tāp	لپ تاپ
to turn on	rowšan kardan	روشن کردن
to turn off	xāmuš kardan	خاموش کردن
keyboard	sahfe kelid	صحفه کلید
key	kelid	کلید
mouse	māows	ماوس
mouse pad	māows pad	ماوس پد
button	dokme	دکمه
cursor	makān namā	مکان نما
monitor	monitor	مونیتور
screen	safhe	صفحه
hard disk	hārd disk	هارد دیسک
hard disk capacity	hajm-e hard	حجم هارد
memory	hāfeze	حافظه
random access memory	hāfeze-ye ram	حافظه رم
file	parvande	پرونده
folder	puše	پوشه
to open (vt)	bāz kardan	باز کردن
to close (vt)	bastan	بستن
to save (vt)	zaxire kardan	ذخیره کردن
to delete (vt)	hazf kardan	حذف کردن
to copy (vt)	kopi kardan	کپی کردن
to sort (vt)	tabaqe bandi kardan	طبقه بندی کردن
to transfer (copy)	kopi kardan	کپی کردن
program	barnāme	برنامه
software	narm afzār	نرم افزار
programmer	barnāme-ye nevis	برنامه نویس
to program (vt)	barnāme-nevisi kardan	برنامه نویسی کردن
hacker	haker	هکر
password	kalame-ye obur	کلمه عبور

| virus | virus | ویروس |
| to find, to detect | peydā kardan | پیدا کردن |

| byte | bāyt | بایت |
| megabyte | megābāyt | مگابایت |

| data | dāde-hā | داده ها |
| database | pāygāh dāde-hā | پایگاه داده ها |

cable (USB, etc.)	kābl	کابل
to disconnect (vt)	jodā kardan	جدا کردن
to connect (sth to sth)	vasl kardan	وصل کردن

140. Internet. E-mail

Internet	internet	اینترنت
browser	morurgar	مرورگر
search engine	motor-e jostoju	موتور جستجو
provider	erāe-ye dehande	ارائه دهنده

webmaster	tarrāh-e vebsāyt	طراح وب سایت
website	veb-sāyt	وب سایت
webpage	safhe-ye veb	صفحه وب

| address (e-mail ~) | nešāni | نشانی |
| address book | daftarče-ye nešāni | دفترچه نشانی |

mailbox	sanduq-e post	صندوق پست
mail	post	پست
full (adj)	por	پر

message	payām	پیام
incoming messages	payāmhā-ye vorudi	پیامهای ورودی
outgoing messages	payāmhā-ye xoruji	پیامهای خروجی

sender	ferestande	فرستنده
to send (vt)	ferestādan	فرستادن
sending (of mail)	ersāl	ارسال

| receiver | girande | گیرنده |
| to receive (vt) | gereftan | گرفتن |

| correspondence | mokātebe | مکاتبه |
| to correspond (vi) | mokātebe kardan | مکاتبه کردن |

file	parvande	پرونده
to download (vt)	dānlod kardan	دانلود کردن
to create (vt)	ijād kardan	ایجاد کردن
to delete (vt)	hazf kardan	حذف کردن
deleted (adj)	hazf šode	حذف شده

connection (ADSL, etc.)	ertebāt	ارتباط
speed	sor'at	سرعت
modem	modem	مودم
access	dastyābi	دستیابی
port (e.g., input ~)	dargāh	درگاه
connection (make a ~)	ertebāt	ارتباط
to connect to … (vi)	vasl šodan	وصل شدن
to select (vt)	entexāb kardan	انتخاب کردن
to search (for …)	jostoju kardan	جستجو کردن

Transportation

141. Airplane

airplane	havāpeymā	هواپیما
air ticket	belit-e havāpeymā	بلیط هواپیما
airline	šerkat-e havāpeymāyi	شرکت هواپیمایی
airport	forudgāh	فرودگاه
supersonic (adj)	māvarā sowt	ماوراء صوت
captain	kāpitān	کاپیتان
crew	xadame	خدمه
pilot	xalabān	خلبان
flight attendant (fem.)	meh-māndār-e havāpeymā	مهماندار هواپیما
navigator	nāvbar	ناوبر
wings	bāl-hā	بال ها
tail	dam	دم
cockpit	kābin	کابین
engine	motor	موتور
undercarriage (landing gear)	šāssi	شاسی
turbine	turbin	توربین
propeller	parvāne	پروانه
black box	ja'be-ye siyāh	جعبه سیاه
yoke (control column)	farmān	فرمان
fuel	suxt	سوخت
safety card	dasturol'amal	دستورالعمل
oxygen mask	māsk-e oksižen	ماسک اکسیژن
uniform	oniform	اونیفورم
life vest	jeliqe-ye nejāt	جلیقۀ نجات
parachute	čatr-e nejāt	چترنجات
takeoff	parvāz	پرواز
to take off (vi)	parvāz kardan	پرواز کردن
runway	bānd-e forudgāh	باند فرودگاه
visibility	meydān did	میدان دید
flight (act of flying)	parvāz	پرواز
altitude	ertefā'	ارتفاع
air pocket	čāle-ye havāyi	چاله هوایی
seat	jā	جا
headphones	guši	گوشی

folding tray (tray table)	sini-ye tāšow	سینی تاشو
airplane window	panjere	پنجره
aisle	rāhrow	راهرو

142. Train

train	qatār	قطار
commuter train	qatār-e barqi	قطار برقی
express train	qatār-e sari'osseyr	قطارسریع السیر
diesel locomotive	lokomotiv-e dizel	لوکوموتیو دیزل
steam locomotive	lokomotiv-e boxar	لوکوموتیو بخار

| passenger car | vāgon | واگن |
| dining car | vāgon-e resturān | واگن رستوران |

rails	reyl-hā	ریل ها
railroad	rāh āhan	راه آهن
railway tie	reyl-e band	ریل بند

platform (railway ~)	sakku-ye rāh-āhan	سکوی راه آهن
track (~ 1, 2, etc.)	masir	مسیر
semaphore	nešanar	نشانبر
station	istgāh	ایستگاه

engineer (train driver)	rānande	راننده
porter (of luggage)	bārbar	باربر
car attendant	rāhnamā-ye qatār	راهنمای قطار
passenger	mosāfer	مسافر
conductor (ticket inspector)	kontorol či	کنترل چی

| corridor (in train) | rāhrow | راهرو |
| emergency brake | tormoz-e ezterāri | ترمز اضطراری |

compartment	kupe	کوپه
berth	taxt-e kupe	تخت کوپه
upper berth	taxt-e bālā	تخت بالا
lower berth	taxt-e pāyin	تخت پایین
bed linen, bedding	raxt-e xāb	رخت خواب

ticket	belit	بلیط
schedule	barnāme	برنامه
information display	barnāme-ye zamāni	برنامه زمانی

to leave, to depart	tark kardan	ترک کردن
departure (of train)	harekat	حرکت
to arrive (ab. train)	residan	رسیدن
arrival	vorud	ورود
to arrive by train	bā qatār āmadan	با قطار آمدن
to get on the train	savār-e qatār šodan	سوار قطار شدن

to get off the train	az catār piyāde šodan	از قطار پیاده شدن
train wreck	sānehe	سانحه
to derail (vi)	az xat xārej šodan	از خط خارج شدن
steam locomotive	lckomotiv-e boxar	لوکوموتیو بخار
stoker, fireman	ātaškār	آتشکار
firebox	ātašdān	آتشدان
coal	zoqāl sang	زغال سنگ

143. Ship

ship	kešti	کشتی
vessel	kešti	کشتی
steamship	kešti-ye boxāri	کشتی بخاری
riverboat	qāyeq-e rudxāne	قایق رودخانه
cruise ship	kešti-ye tafrihi	کشتی تفریحی
cruiser	razm nāv	رزم ناو
yacht	qāyeq-e tafrihi	قایق تفریحی
tugboat	yadak keš	یدک کش
barge	kešti-ye bārkeše yadaki	کشتی بارکش یدکی
ferry	kešti-ye farābar	کشتی فرابر
sailing ship	kešti-ye bādbāni	کشتی بادبانی
brigantine	košti dozdān daryā-yi	کشتی دزدان دریایی
ice breaker	kešti-ye yaxšekan	کشتی یخ شکن
submarine	zirdaryāyi	زیردریایی
boat (flat-bottomed ~)	qāyeq	قایق
dinghy	qāyeq-e tafrihi	قایق تفریحی
lifeboat	qāyeq-e nejāt	قایق نجات
motorboat	qāyeq-e motori	قایق موتوری
captain	kāpitān	کاپیتان
seaman	malavān	ملوان
sailor	malavān	ملوان
crew	xadame	خدمه
boatswain	sar malavān	سر ملوان
ship's boy	šāgerd-e malavān	شاگرد ملوان
cook	āšpaz-e kešti	آشپز کشتی
ship's doctor	pezešk-e kešti	پزشک کشتی
deck	arše-ye kešti	عرشهٔ کشتی
mast	dakal	دکل
sail	bādbān	بادبان
hold	anbār	انبار
bow (prow)	sine-ye kešti	سینه کشتی

stern	aqab kešti	عقب کشتی
oar	pāru	پارو
screw propeller	parvāne	پروانه
cabin	otāq-e kešti	اتاق کشتی
wardroom	otāq-e afsarān	اتاق افسران
engine room	motor xāne	موتور خانه
bridge	pol-e farmāndehi	پل فرماندهی
radio room	kābin-e bisim	کابین بی سیم
wave (radio)	mowj	موج
logbook	roxdād nāme	رخداد نامه
spyglass	teleskop	تلسکوپ
bell	nāqus	ناقوس
flag	parčam	پرچم
hawser (mooring ~)	tanāb	طناب
knot (bowline, etc.)	gereh	گره
deckrails	narde	نرده
gangway	pol	پل
anchor	langar	لنگر
to weigh anchor	langar kešidan	لنگر کشیدن
to drop anchor	langar andāxtan	لنگر انداختن
anchor chain	zanjir-e langar	زنجیر لنگر
port (harbor)	bandar	بندر
quay, wharf	eskele	اسکله
to berth (moor)	pahlu gereftan	پهلو گرفتن
to cast off	tark kardan	ترک کردن
trip, voyage	mosāferat	مسافرت
cruise (sea trip)	safar-e daryāyi	سفر دریایی
course (route)	masir	مسیر
route (itinerary)	masir	مسیر
fairway (safe water channel)	kešti-ye ru	کشتی رو
shallows	mahall-e kam omq	محل کم عمق
to run aground	be gel nešastan	به گل نشستن
storm	tufān	طوفان
signal	alāmat	علامت
to sink (vi)	qarq šodan	غرق شدن
Man overboard!	kas-i dar hāl-e qarq šodan-ast!	کسی در حال غرق شدن است!
SOS (distress signal)	sos	SOS
ring buoy	kamarband-e nejāt	کمربند نجات

144. Airport

airport	forudgāh	فرودگاه
airplane	havāpeymā	هواپیما
airline	šerkat-e havāpeymāyi	شرکت هواپیمایی
air traffic controller	ma'mur-e kontorol-e terāfik-e havāyi	مأمور کنترل ترافیک هوایی
departure	azimat	عزیمت
arrival	vorud	ورود
to arrive (by plane)	residan	رسیدن
departure time	zamān-e parvāz	زمان پرواز
arrival time	zamān-e vorud	زمان ورود
to be delayed	ta'xir kardan	تأخیر کردن
flight delay	ta'xir-e parvāz	تأخیر پرواز
information board	tāblo-ye ettelā'āt	تابلوی اطلاعات
information	ettelā'āt	اطلاعات
to announce (vt)	e'lām kardan	اعلام کردن
flight (e.g., next ~)	parvāz	پرواز
customs	gomrok	گمرک
customs officer	ma'mur-e gomrok	مأمور گمرک
customs declaration	ežhār-nāme	اظهارنامه
to fill out (vt)	por kardan	پر کردن
to fill out the declaration	ežhār-nāme rā por kardan	اظهارنامه را پر کردن
passport control	kontorol-e gozarnāme	کنترل گذرنامه
luggage	bār	بار
hand luggage	bār-e dasti	بار دستی
luggage cart	čarx-e hamle bar	چرخ حمل بار
landing	forud	فرود
landing strip	bānd-e forudgāh	باند فرودگاه
to land (vi)	nešastan	نشستن
airstairs	pellekān	پلکان
check-in	ček in	چک این
check-in counter	bāje-ye kontorol	باجه کنترل
to check-in (vi)	čekin kardan	چکاین کردن
boarding pass	kārt-e parvāz	کارت پرواز
departure gate	gi-yat xoruj	گیت خروج
transit	terānzit	ترانزیت
to wait (vt)	montazer budan	منتظر بودن
departure lounge	tālār-e entezār	تالار انتظار
to see off	badraqe kardan	بدرقه کردن
to say goodbye	xodāhāfezi kardan	خداحافظی کردن

145. Bicycle. Motorcycle

bicycle	dočarxe	دوچرخه
scooter	eskuter	اسکوتر
motorcycle, bike	motorsiklet	موتورسیکلت

to go by bicycle	bā dočarxe raftan	با دوچرخه رفتن
handlebars	farmān-e dočarxe	فرمان دوچرخه
pedal	pedāl	پدال
brakes	tormoz	ترمز
bicycle seat (saddle)	zin	زین

pump	pomp	پمپ
luggage rack	tarakband	ترکبند
front lamp	čerāq-e jelo	چراغ جلو
helmet	kolāh-e imeni	کلاه ایمنی

wheel	čarx	چرخ
fender	golgir	گلگیر
rim	towqe	طوقه
spoke	parre	پره

Cars

146. Types of cars

automobile, car	otomobil	اتومبیل
sports car	otomobil-e varzeši	اتومبیل ورزشی
limousine	limozin	لیموزین
off-road vehicle	jip	جیپ
convertible (n)	kābriyole	کابریولیه
minibus	mini bus	مینی بوس
ambulance	āmbolāns	آمبولانس
snowplow	māšin-e barfrub	ماشین برف روب
truck	kāmiyon	کامیون
tanker truck	tānker	تانکر
van (small truck)	kāmiyon	کامیون
road tractor (trailer truck)	tereyler	تریلر
trailer	yadak	یدک
comfortable (adj)	rāhat	راحت
used (adj)	dast-e dovvom	دست دوم

147. Cars. Bodywork

hood	kāput	کاپوت
fender	golgir	گلگیر
roof	saqf	سقف
windshield	šiše-ye jelo	شیشه جلو
rear-view mirror	āyene-ye did-e aqab	آینه دید عقب
windshield washer	pak konande	پاک کننده
windshield wipers	barf pāk kon	برف پاک کن
side window	šiše-ye baqal	شیشهٔ بغل
window lift (power window)	šiše bālābar	شیشه بالابر
antenna	ānten	آنتن
sunroof	sanrof	سانروف
bumper	separ	سپر
trunk	sanduq-e aqab	صندوق عقب
roof luggage rack	bārband	باربند
door	darb	درب

| door handle | dastgire-ye dar | دستگیرهٔ در |
| door lock | qofl | قفل |

license plate	pelāk	پلاک
muffler	xafe kon	خفه کن
gas tank	bāk-e benzin	باک بنزین
tailpipe	lule-ye egzoz	لولهٔ اگزوز

gas, accelerator	gāz	گاز
pedal	pedāl	پدال
gas pedal	pedāl-e gāz	پدال گاز

| brake | tormoz | ترمز |
| brake pedal | pedāl-e tormoz | پدال ترمز |

| to brake (use the brake) | tormoz kardan | ترمز کردن |
| parking brake | tormoz-e dasti | ترمز دستی |

| clutch | kelāč | کلاچ |
| clutch pedal | pedāl-e kelāč | پدال کلاچ |

| clutch disc | disk-e kelāč | دیسک کلاچ |
| shock absorber | komak-e fanar | کمک فنر |

wheel	čarx	چرخ
spare tire	zāpās	زاپاس
hubcap	qālpāq	قالپاق

| driving wheels | čarxhā-ye moharrek | چرخ های محرک |
| front-wheel drive (as adj) | mehvarhā-ye jelo | محورهای جلو |

| rear-wheel drive (as adj) | mehvarhā-ye aqab | محورهای عقب |
| all-wheel drive (as adj) | tamām-e čarx | تمام چرخ |

| gearbox | ja'be-ye dande | جعبهٔ دنده |
| automatic (adj) | otumātik | اتوماتیک |

| mechanical (adj) | mekāniki | مکانیکی |
| gear shift | ahrom-e ja'be dande | اهرم جعبه دنده |

| headlight | čerāq-e jelo | چراغ جلو |
| headlights | čerāq-hā | چراغ ها |

low beam	nur-e pāin	نور پائین
high beam	nur-e bālā	نور بالا
brake light	čerāq-e tormoz	چراغ ترمز

parking lights	čerāqhā-ye pārk	چراغ های پارک
hazard lights	čerāqha-ye xatar	چراغ های خطر
fog lights	čerāqhā-ye meh-e šekan	چراغ های مه شکن
turn signal	čerāq-e rāhnamā	چراغ راهنما
back-up light	čerāq-e dande-ye aqab	چراغ دنده عقب

148. Cars. Passenger compartment

car inside (interior)	dāxel-e xodrow	داخل خودرو
leather (as adj)	čarmi	چرمی
velour (as adj)	maxmali	مخملی
upholstery	tuduzi	تودوزی
instrument (gage)	abzār	ابزار
dashboard	safhe-ye dāšbord	صفحه داشبورد
speedometer	sor'at sanj	سرعت سنج
needle (pointer)	aqrabe	عقربه
odometer	kilumetr-e šomār	کیلومتر شمار
indicator (sensor)	nešāngar	نشانگر
level	sath	سطح
warning light	lāmp	لامپ
steering wheel	farmān	فرمان
horn	buq	بوق
button	dokme	دکمه
switch	kelid	کلید
seat	sandali	صندلی
backrest	pošti-ye sandali	پشتی صندلی
headrest	zir-e seri	زیر سری
seat belt	kamarband-e imeni	کمربند ایمنی
to fasten the belt	kamarband rā bastan	کمربند را بستن
adjustment (of seats)	tanzim	تنظیم
airbag	kise-ye havā	کیسه هوا
air-conditioner	tahviye-ye matbu'	تهویه مطبوع
radio	rādiyo	رادیو
CD player	paxš konande-ye si di	پخش کننده سی دی
to turn on	rowšan kardan	روشن کردن
antenna	ānten	آنتن
glove box	dāšbord	داشبورد
ashtray	zir-sigāri	زیرسیگاری

149. Cars. Engine

engine, motor	motor	موتور
diesel (as adj)	dizel	دیزل
gasoline (as adj)	benzin	بنزین
engine volume	hajm-e motor	حجم موتور
power	niru	نیرو
horsepower	asb-e boxār	اسب بخار
piston	pistun	پیستون

| cylinder | silandr | سیلندر |
| valve | supāp | سوپاپ |

injector	anžektor	انژکتور
generator (alternator)	ženerātor	ژنراتور
carburetor	kārborātor	کاربراتور
motor oil	rowqan-e motor	روغن موتور

radiator	rādiyātor	رادیاتور
coolant	māye-'e sard konande	مایع سرد کننده
cooling fan	fan-e xonak konande	فن خنک کننده

battery (accumulator)	bātri-ye māšin	باتری ماشین
starter	estārt	استارت
ignition	ehterāq	احتراق
spark plug	šam'-e motor	شمع موتور

terminal (of battery)	pāyāne	پایانه
positive terminal	mosbat	مثبت
negative terminal	manfi	منفی
fuse	fiyuz	فیوز

air filter	filter-e havā	فیلتر هوا
oil filter	filter-e rowqan	فیلتر روغن
fuel filter	filter-e suxt	فیلتر سوخت

150. Cars. Crash. Repair

car crash	tasādof	تصادف
traffic accident	tasādof	تصادف
to crash (into the wall, etc.)	barxord kardan	برخورد کردن

to get smashed up	tasādof kardan	تصادف کردن
damage	āsib	آسیب
intact (unscathed)	sālem	سالم

breakdown	xarābi	خرابی
to break down (vi)	xarāb šodan	خراب شدن
towrope	sim-e boksel	سیم بکسل

puncture	pančar	پنجر
to be flat	pančar šodan	پنجر شدن
to pump up	bād kardan	باد کردن
pressure	fešār	فشار
to check (to examine)	barresi kardan	بررسی کردن

repair	ta'mir	تعمیر
auto repair shop	ta'mirgāh-e xodro	تعمیرگاه خودرو
spare part	qet'e-ye yadaki	قطعه یدکی
part	qet'e	قطعه

bolt (with nut)	pič	پیچ
screw (fastener)	pič	پیچ
nut	mohre	مهره
washer	vāšer	واشر
bearing	yātāqān	یاتاقان
tube	lule	لوله
gasket (head ~)	vāšer	واشر
cable, wire	sim	سیم
jack	jak	جک
wrench	āčār	آچار
hammer	čakoš	چکش
pump	pomp	پمپ
screwdriver	pič gušti	پیچ گوشتی
fire extinguisher	kapsul-e ātašnešāni	کپسول آتش نشانی
warning triangle	alāmat-e ehtiyāt	علامت احتیاط
to stall (vi)	xāmuš šodan	خاموش شدن
stall (n)	tavaqqof	توقف
to be broken	xarāb budan	خراب بودن
to overheat (vi)	juš āvardan	جوش آوردن
to be clogged up	masdud šodan	مسدود شدن
to freeze up (pipes, etc.)	yax bastan	یخ بستن
to burst (vi, ab. tube)	tarakidan	ترکیدن
pressure	fešār	فشار
level	sath	سطح
slack (~ belt)	za'if	ضعیف
dent	foruraftegi	فرورفتگی
knocking noise (engine)	sedā	صدا
crack	tarak	ترک
scratch	xarāš	خراش

151. Cars. Road

road	rāh	راه
highway	bozorgrāh	بزرگراه
freeway	āzād-e rāh	آزاد راه
direction (way)	samt	سمت
distance	masāfat	مسافت
bridge	pol	پل
parking lot	pārking	پارکینگ
square	meydān	میدان
interchange	dowr bargardān	دوربرگردان
tunnel	tunel	تونل

gas station	pomp-e benzin	پمپ بنزین
parking lot	pārking	پارکینگ
gas pump (fuel dispenser)	pomp-e benzin	پمپ بنزین
auto repair shop	ta'mirgāh-e xodro	تعمیرگاه خودرو
to get gas (to fill up)	benzin zadan	بنزین زدن
fuel	suxt	سوخت
jerrycan	dabbe	دبه
asphalt	āsfālt	آسفالت
road markings	alāmat-e gozari	علامت گذاری
curb	labe-ye jadval	لبه جدول
guardrail	narde	نرده
ditch	juy	جوی
roadside (shoulder)	kenār rāh	کنار راه
lamppost	tir-e barq	تیر برق
to drive (a car)	rāndan	راندن
to turn (e.g., ~ left)	pičidan	پیچیدن
to make a U-turn	dowr zadan	دور زدن
reverse (~ gear)	dande aqab	دنده عقب
to honk (vi)	buq zadan	بوق زدن
honk (sound)	buq	بوق
to get stuck (in the mud, etc.)	gir kardan	گیر کردن
to spin the wheels	sor xordan	سر خوردن
to cut, to turn off (vt)	xāmuš kardan	خاموش کردن
speed	sor'at	سرعت
to exceed the speed limit	az sor'at-e mojāz gozāštan	ازسرعت مجاز گذشتن
to give a ticket	jarime kardan	جریمه کردن
traffic lights	čerāq-e rāhnamā	چراغ راهنما
driver's license	govāhi-nāme-ye rānandegi	گواهینامة رانندگی
grade crossing	taqāto'	تقاطع
intersection	čahārrāh	چهارراه
crosswalk	xatt-e āber-e piyāde	خط عابرپیاده
bend, curve	pič	پیچ
pedestrian zone	mantaqe-ye āber-e piyāde	منطقة عابر پیاده

PEOPLE. LIFE EVENTS

Life events

152. Holidays. Event

celebration, holiday	jašn	جشن
national day	eyd-e melli	عید ملی
public holiday	ruz-e jašn	روز جشن
to commemorate (vt)	jašn gereftan	جشن گرفتن
event (happening)	vāqe'e	واقعه
event (organized activity)	ruydād	رویداد
banquet (party)	ziyāfat	ضیافت
reception (formal party)	ziyāfat	ضیافت
feast	jašn	جشن
anniversary	sālgard	سالگرد
jubilee	sālgard	سالگرد
to celebrate (vt)	jašn gereftan	جشن گرفتن
New Year	sāl-e now	سال نو
Happy New Year!	sāl-e now mobārak	سال نو مبارک
Santa Claus	bābā noel	بابا نوئل
Christmas	kerismas	کریسمس
Merry Christmas!	kərismas mobārak!	کریسمس مبارک!
Christmas tree	kāj kerismas	کاج کریسمس
fireworks (fireworks show)	ātaš-e bāzi	آتش بازی
wedding	arusi	عروسی
groom	dāmād	داماد
bride	arus	عروس
to invite (vt)	da'vat kardan	دعوت کردن
invitation card	da'vatnāme	دعوتنامه
guest	mehmān	مهمان
to visit	be mehmāni raftan	به مهمانی رفتن
(~ your parents, etc.)		
to meet the guests	az mehmānān esteqbāl kardan	از مهمانان استقبال کردن
gift, present	hedye	هدیه
to give (sth as present)	hadye dādan	هدیه دادن

| to receive gifts | hediye gereftan | هدیه گرفتن |
| bouquet (of flowers) | daste-ye gol | دسته گل |

| congratulations | tabrik | تبریک |
| to congratulate (vt) | tabrik goftan | تبریک گفتن |

greeting card	kārt-e tabrik	کارت تبریک
to send a postcard	kārt-e tabrik ferestādan	کارت تبریک فرستادن
to get a postcard	kārt-e tabrik gereftan	کارت تبریک گرفتن

| toast | be salāmati-ye kas-i nušidan | به سلامتی کسی نوشیدن |

| to offer (a drink, etc.) | pazirāyi kardan | پذیرایی کردن |
| champagne | šāmpāyn | شامپاین |

to enjoy oneself	šādi kardan	شادی کردن
merriment (gaiety)	šādi	شادی
joy (emotion)	maserrat	مسرت

| dance | raqs | رقص |
| to dance (vi, vt) | raqsidan | رقصیدن |

| waltz | raqs-e vāls | رقص والس |
| tango | raqs tāngo | رقص تانگو |

153. Funerals. Burial

cemetery	qabrestān	قبرستان
grave, tomb	qabr	قبر
cross	salib	صلیب
gravestone	sang-e qabr	سنگ قبر
fence	hesār	حصار
chapel	kelisā-ye kučak	کلیسای کوچک

death	marg	مرگ
to die (vi)	mordan	مردن
the deceased	marhum	مرحوم
mourning	azā	عزا

to bury (vt)	dafn kardan	دفن کردن
funeral home	xadamat-e kafno dafn	خدمات کفن ودفن
funeral	tašyi-'e jenāze	تشییع جنازه

wreath	tāj-e gol	تاج گل
casket, coffin	tābut	تابوت
hearse	na'š keš	نعش کش
shroud	kafan	کفن

| funeral procession | tašyi-'e jenāze | تشییع جنازه |
| funerary urn | zarf-e xākestar-e morde | ظرف خاکستر مرده |

crematory	morde suz xāne	مرده سوز خانه
obituary	āgahi-ye tarhim	آگهی ترحیم
to cry (weep)	gerye kardan	گریه کردن
to sob (vi)	zār zār gerye kardan	زار زارگریه کردن

154. War. Soldiers

platoon	daste	دسته
company	goruhān	گروهان
regiment	hang	هنگ
army	arteš	ارتش
division	laškar	لشکر

| section, squad | daste | دسته |
| host (army) | laškar | لشکر |

| soldier | sarbāz | سرباز |
| officer | afsar | افسر |

private	sarbāz	سرباز
sergeant	goruhbān	گروهبان
lieutenant	sotvān	ستوان
captain	kāpitān	کاپیتان
major	sargord	سرگرد
colonel	sarhang	سرهنگ
general	ženerāl	ژنرال

sailor	malavān	ملوان
captain	kāpitān	کاپیتان
boatswain	sar malavān	سر ملوان

artilleryman	tupči	توپچی
paratrooper	sarbāz-e čatrbāz	سرباز چترباز
pilot	xalabān	خلبان
navigator	nāvbar	ناوبر
mechanic	mekānik	مکانیک

pioneer (sapper)	mohandes estehkāmāt	مهندس استحکامات
parachutist	čatr bāz	چترباز
reconnaissance scout	ettelā'āti	اطلاعاتی
sniper	tak tir andāz	تک تیر انداز

patrol (group)	gašt	گشت
to patrol (vt)	gašt zadan	گشت زدن
sentry, guard	negahbān	نگهبان

warrior	jangju	جنگجو
patriot	mihan parast	میهن پرست
hero	qahremān	قهرمان
heroine	qahremān-e zan	قهرمان زن

| traitor | xāen | خائن |
| to betray (vt) | xiyānat kardan | خیانت کردن |

| deserter | farāri | فراری |
| to desert (vi) | farāri budan | فراری بودن |

mercenary	mozdur	مزدور
recruit	sarbāz-e jadid	سرباز جدید
volunteer	dāvtalab	داوطلب

dead (n)	morde	مرده
wounded (n)	zaxmi	زخمی
prisoner of war	asir	اسیر

155. War. Military actions. Part 1

war	jang	جنگ
to be at war	jangidan	جنگیدن
civil war	jang-e dāxeli	جنگ داخلی

treacherously (adv)	xāenāne	خائنانه
declaration of war	e'lān-e jang	اعلان جنگ
to declare (~ war)	e'lān kardan	اعلان کردن
aggression	tajāvoz	تجاوز
to attack (invade)	hamle kardan	حمله کردن

to invade (vt)	tajāvoz kardan	تجاوز کردن
invader	tajāvozgar	تجاوزگر
conqueror	fāteh	فاتح

defense	defā'	دفاع
to defend (a country, etc.)	defā' kardan	دفاع کردن
to defend (against ...)	az xod defā' kardan	از خود دفاع کردن

enemy	došman	دشمن
foe, adversary	moxālef	مخالف
enemy (as adj)	došman	دشمن

| strategy | rāhbord | راهبرد |
| tactics | tāktik | تاکتیک |

order	farmān	فرمان
command (order)	dastur	دستور
to order (vt)	farmān dādan	فرمان دادن
mission	ma'muriyat	مأموریت
secret (adj)	mahramāne	محرمانه

battle	jang	جنگ
combat	nabard	نبرد
attack	hamle	حمله

charge (assault)	yureš	یورش
to storm (vt)	yureš bordan	یورش بردن
siege (to be under ~)	mohāsere	محاصره
offensive (n)	hamle	حمله
to go on the offensive	hamle kardan	حمله کردن
retreat	aqab nešini	عقب نشینی
to retreat (vi)	ɛqab nešini kardan	عقب نشینی کردن
encirclement	mohāsere	محاصره
to encircle (vt)	mohāsere kardan	محاصره کردن
bombing (by aircraft)	bombārān-e havāyi	بمباران هوایی
to drop a bomb	bomb āndaxtan	بمب انداختن
to bomb (vt)	bombārān kardan	بمباران کردن
explosion	enfejār	انفجار
shot	tirandāzi	تیراندازی
to fire (~ a shot)	tirandāzi kardan	تیراندازی کردن
firing (burst of ~)	tirandāzi	تیراندازی
to aim (to point a weapon)	nešāne raftan	نشانه رفتن
to point (a gun)	šellik kardan	شلیک کردن
to hit (the target)	residan	رسیدن
to sink (~ a ship)	qarq šodan	غرق شدن
hole (in a ship)	surāx	سوراخ
to founder, to sink (vi)	qarq šodan	غرق شدن
front (war ~)	jebhe	جبهه
evacuation	taxliye	تخلیه
to evacuate (vt)	taxliye kardan	تخلیه کردن
trench	sangar	سنگر
barbwire	sim-e xārdār	سیم خاردار
barrier (anti tank ~)	hesār	حصار
watchtower	borj	برج
military hospital	bimārestān-e nezāmi	بیمارستان نظامی
to wound (vt)	majruh kardan	مجروح کردن
wound	zaxm	زخم
wounded (n)	zaxmi	زخمی
to be wounded	zaxmi šodan	زخمی شدن
serious (wound)	zaxm-e saxt	زخم سخت

156. Weapons

weapons	selāh	سلاح
firearms	aslahe-ye garm	اسلحهٔ گرم

cold weapons (knives, etc.)	aslahe-ye sard	اسلحهٔ سرد
chemical weapons	taslihāt-e šimiyāyi	تسلیحات شیمیایی
nuclear (adj)	haste i	هسته ای
nuclear weapons	taslihāt-e hastei	تسلیحات هسته ای
bomb	bomb	بمب
atomic bomb	bomb-e atomi	بمب اتمی
pistol (gun)	kolt	کلت
rifle	tofang	تفنگ
submachine gun	mosalsal-e xodkār	مسلسل خودکار
machine gun	mosalsal	مسلسل
muzzle	sar-e lule-ye tofang	سر لوله تفنگ
barrel	lule-ye tofang	لوله تفنگ
caliber	kālibr	کالیبر
trigger	māše	ماشه
sight (aiming device)	nešāne ravi	نشانه روی
magazine	xešāb	خشاب
butt (shoulder stock)	qondāq	قنداق
hand grenade	nārenjak	نارنجک
explosive	mādde-ye monfajere	مادهٔ منفجره
bullet	golule	گلوله
cartridge	fešang	فشنگ
charge	mohemmāt	مهمات
ammunition	mohemmāt	مهمات
bomber (aircraft)	bomb-afkan	بمبافکن
fighter	jangande	جنگنده
helicopter	helikopter	هلیکوپتر
anti-aircraft gun	tup-e zedd-e havāyi	توپ ضد هوایی
tank	tānk	تانک
tank gun	tup	توپ
artillery	tupxāne	توپخانه
gun (cannon, howitzer)	tofang	تفنگ
to lay (a gun)	šellik kardan	شلیک کردن
shell (projectile)	xompāre	خمپاره
mortar bomb	xompāre	خمپاره
mortar	xompāre andāz	خمپاره انداز
splinter (shell fragment)	tarkeš	ترکش
submarine	zirdaryāyi	زیردریایی
torpedo	eždar	اژدر
missile	mušak	موشک
to load (gun)	por kardan	پر کردن

to shoot (vi)	irandāzi kardan	تیراندازی کردن
to point at (the cannon)	nešāne raftan	نشانه رفتن
bayonet	sarneyze	سرنیزه

rapier	šamšir	شمشیر
saber (e.g., cavalry ~)	šamšir	شمشیر
spear (weapon)	neyze	نیزه
bow	kamān	کمان
arrow	tir	تیر
musket	tofang fetile-i	تفنگ فتیله‌ای
crossbow	kamān zanburak-i	کمان زنبورکی

157. Ancient people

primitive (prehistoric)	avvaliye	اولیه
prehistoric (adj)	piš az tārix	پیش از تاریخ
ancient (~ civilization)	qadimi	قدیمی

Stone Age	asr-e hajar	عصر حجر
Bronze Age	asr-e mafraq	عصر مفرغ
Ice Age	dcwre-ye yaxbandān	دورهٔ یخبندان

tribe	qabile	قبیله
cannibal	ādam xār	آدم خوار
hunter	šekārči	شکارچی
to hunt (vi, vt)	šekār kardan	شکار کردن
mammoth	māmut	ماموت

cave	qār	غار
fire	ātaš	آتش
campfire	ātaš	آتش
cave painting	qār negāre	غار نگاره

tool (e.g., stone ax)	abzār-e kār	ابزار کار
spear	neyze	نیزه
stone ax	tabar-e sangi	تبر سنگی
to be at war	jangidan	جنگیدن
to domesticate (vt)	rām kardan	رام کردن

idol	bot	بت
to worship (vt)	parastidan	پرستیدن
superstition	xorāfe	خرافه
rite	marāsem	مراسم

evolution	takāmol	تکامل
development	pišraft	پیشرفت
disappearance (extinction)	enqerāz	انقراض
to adapt oneself	sāzgār šodan	سازگار شدن
archeology	bāstān-šenāsi	باستان شناسی
archeologist	bāstān-šenās	باستان شناس

archeological (adj)	bāstān-šenāsi	باستان شناسی
excavation site	mahall-e haffārihā	محل حفاری ها
excavations	haffāri-hā	حفاری ها
find (object)	yāfteh	یافته
fragment	qet'e	قطعه

158. Middle Ages

people (ethnic group)	mellat	ملت
peoples	mellat-hā	ملت ها
tribe	qabile	قبیله
tribes	qabāyel	قبایل

barbarians	barbar-hā	بربر ها
Gauls	gul-hā	گول ها
Goths	gat-hā	گت ها
Slavs	eslāv-hā	اسلاو ها
Vikings	vāyking-hā	وایکینگ ها

| Romans | rumi-hā | رومی ها |
| Roman (adj) | rumi | رومی |

Byzantines	bizānsi-hā	بیزانسی ها
Byzantium	bizāns	بیزانس
Byzantine (adj)	bizānsi	بیزانسی

emperor	emperātur	امپراطور
leader, chief (tribal ~)	rahbar	رهبر
powerful (~ king)	moqtader	مقتدر
king	šāh	شاه
ruler (sovereign)	hākem	حاکم

knight	šovālie	شوالیه
feudal lord	feodāl	فئودال
feudal (adj)	feodāli	فئودالی
vassal	ra'yat	رعیت

duke	duk	دوک
earl	kont	کنت
baron	bāron	بارون
bishop	osqof	اسقف

armor	zereh	زره
shield	separ	سپر
sword	šamšir	شمشیر
visor	labe-ye kolāh	لبه کلاه
chainmail	jowšan	جوشن

| Crusade | jang-e salibi | جنگ صلیبی |
| crusader | jangju-ye salibi | جنگجوی صلیبی |

territory	qalamrow	قلمرو
to attack (invade)	hamle kardan	حمله کردن
to conquer (vt)	fath kardan	فتح کردن
to occupy (invade)	ešqāl kardan	اشغال کردن

siege (to be under ~)	mohāsere	محاصره
besieged (adj)	mahsur	محصور
to besiege (vt)	mohāsere kardan	محاصره کردن

inquisition	taftiš-e aqāyed	تفتیش عقاید
inquisitor	mofatteš	مفتش
torture	šekanje	شکنجه
cruel (adj)	bi rahm	بی رحم
heretic	molhed	ملحد
heresy	ertedād	ارتداد

seafaring	daryānavardi	دریانوردی
pirate	dozd-e daryāyi	دزد دریایی
piracy	dozdi-ye daryāyi	دزدی دریایی
boarding (attack)	hamle ruye arše	حمله روی عرشه
loot, booty	qanimat	غنیمت
treasures	ganj	گنج

discovery	kašf	کشف
to discover (new land, etc.)	kašf kardan	کشف کردن
expedition	safar	سفر

musketeer	tofangdār	تفنگدار
cardinal	kārdināl	کاردینال
heraldry	nešān-šenāsi	نشان شناسی
heraldic (adj)	manquš	منقوش

159. Leader. Chief. Authorities

king	šāh	شاه
queen	maleke	ملکه
royal (adj)	šāhi	شاهی
kingdom	pādšāhi	پادشاهی

| prince | šāhzāde | شاهزاده |
| princess | pranses | پرنسس |

president	ra'is jomhur	رئیس جمهور
vice-president	mo'āven-e rais-e jomhur	معاون رئیس جمهور
senator	senātor	سناتور

monarch	pādšāh	پادشاه
ruler (sovereign)	hākem	حاکم
dictator	diktātor	دیکتاتور
tyrant	zālem	ظالم

magnate	najib zāde	نجيب زاده
director	modir	مدير
chief	ra'is	رئيس
manager (director)	modir	مدير
boss	ra'is	رئيس
owner	sāheb	صاحب

leader	rahbar	رهبر
head (~ of delegation)	ra'is	رئيس
authorities	maqāmāt	مقامات
superiors	roasā	رؤسا

governor	farmāndār	فرماندار
consul	konsul	کنسول
diplomat	diplomāt	ديپلمات
mayor	šahrdār	شهردار
sheriff	kalāntar	کلانتر

emperor	emperātur	امپراطور
tsar, czar	tezār	تزار
pharaoh	fer'own	فرعون
khan	xān	خان

160. Breaking the law. Criminals. Part 1

bandit	rāhzan	راهزن
crime	jenāyat	جنايت
criminal (person)	jenāyatkār	جنايتکار

thief	dozd	دزد
to steal (vi, vt)	dozdidan	دزديدن
stealing (larceny)	dozdi	دزدی
theft	serqat	سرقت

to kidnap (vt)	ādam robudan	آدم ربودن
kidnapping	ādam robāyi	آدم ربايی
kidnapper	ādam robā	آدم ربا

| ransom | bāj | باج |
| to demand ransom | bāj xāstan | باج خواستن |

to rob (vt)	serqat kardan	سرقت کردن
robbery	serqat	سرقت
robber	qāratgar	غارتگر

to extort (vt)	axxāzi kardan	اخاذی کردن
extortionist	axxāz	اخاذ
extortion	axxāzi	اخاذی
to murder, to kill	koštan	کشتن
murder	qatl	قتل

murderer	qātel	قاتل
gunshot	tirandāzi	تیراندازی
to fire (~ a shot)	tirandāzi kardan	تیراندازی کردن
to shoot to death	bā tir zadan	با تیر زدن
to shoot (vi)	tirandāzi kardan	تیراندازی کردن
shooting	tirandāzi	تیراندازی

incident (fight, etc.)	vāqe'e	واقعه
fight, brawl	zad-o xord	زد و خورد
Help!	komak!	کمک!
victim	qorbāni	قربانی

to damage (vt)	xesārat resāndan	خسارت رساندن
damage	xesārat	خسارت
dead body, corpse	jasad	جسد
grave (~ crime)	vaxim	وخیم

to attack (vt)	hamle kardan	حمله کردن
to beat (to hit)	zadan	زدن
to beat up	kotak zadan	کتک زدن
to take (rob of sth)	bezur gereftan	به زور گرفتن
to stab to death	čāqu zadan	چاقو زدن
to maim (vt)	ma'yub kardan	معیوب کردن
to wound (vt)	majruh kardan	مجروح کردن

blackmail	šāntāž	شانتاژ
to blackmail (vt)	axxāzi kardan	اخاذی کردن
blackmailer	axxāz	اخاذ

protection racket	axxāzi	اخاذی
racketeer	axxāz	اخاذ
gangster	gāngester	گانگستر
mafia, Mob	māfiyā	مافیا

pickpocket	jib bor	جیب بر
burglar	sāreq	سارق
smuggling	qāčāq	قاچاق
smuggler	qāčāqči	قاچاقچی

forgery	qollābi	قلابی
to forge (counterfeit)	ja'l kardan	جعل کردن
fake (forged)	ja'li	جعلی

161. Breaking the law. Criminals. Part 2

rape	tajāvoz be nāmus	تجاوز به ناموس
to rape (vt)	tajāvoz kardan	تجاوز کردن
rapist	zenā konande	زنا کننده
maniac	majnun	مجنون
prostitute (fem.)	fāheše	فاحشه

prostitution	fāhešegi	فاحشگی
pimp	jākeš	جاکش
drug addict	mo'tād	معتاد
drug dealer	forušande-ye mavādd-e moxadder	فروشندهٔ مواد مخدر
to blow up (bomb)	monfajer kardan	منفجر کردن
explosion	enfejār	انفجار
to set fire	ātaš zadan	آتش زدن
arsonist	ātaš afruz	آتش افروز
terrorism	terorism	تروریسم
terrorist	terorist	تروریست
hostage	gerowgān	گروگان
to swindle (deceive)	farib dādan	فریب دادن
swindle, deception	farib	فریب
swindler	hoqqe bāz	حقه باز
to bribe (vt)	rešve dādan	رشوه دادن
bribery	rešve	رشوه
bribe	rešve	رشوه
poison	zahr	زهر
to poison (vt)	masmum kardan	مسموم کردن
to poison oneself	masmum šodan	مسموم شدن
suicide (act)	xod-koši	خودکشی
suicide (person)	xod-koši konande	خودکشی کننده
to threaten (vt)	tahdid kardan	تهدید کردن
threat	tahdid	تهدید
to make an attempt	su'-e qasd kardan	سوء قصد کردن
attempt (attack)	su'-e qasd	سوء قصد
to steal (a car)	robudan	ربودن
to hijack (a plane)	havāpeymā robāyi	هواپیما ربایی
revenge	enteqām	انتقام
to avenge (get revenge)	enteqām gereftan	انتقام گرفتن
to torture (vt)	šekanje dādan	شکنجه دادن
torture	šekanje	شکنجه
to torment (vt)	aziyat kardan	اذیت کردن
pirate	dozd-e daryāyi	دزد دریایی
hooligan	owbāš	اوباش
armed (adj)	mosallah	مسلح
violence	xošunat	خشونت
illegal (unlawful)	qeyr-e qānuni	غیر قانونی
spying (espionage)	jāsusi	جاسوسی
to spy (vi)	jāsusi kardan	جاسوسی کردن

162. Police. Law. Part 1

| justice | edālat | عدالت |
| court (see you in ~) | dādgāh | دادگاه |

judge	qāzi	قاضی
jurors	hey'at-e monsefe	هیئت منصفه
jury trial	hey'at-e monsefe	هیئت منصفه
to judge (vt)	mohākeme kardan	محاکمه کردن

lawyer, attorney	vakil	وکیل
defendant	mottaham	متهم
dock	jāygāh-e mottaham	جایگاه متهم

| charge | ettehām | اتهام |
| accused | mottaham | متهم |

| sentence | hokm | حکم |
| to sentence (vt) | mahkum kardan | محکوم کردن |

guilty (culprit)	moqasser	مقصر
to punish (vt)	mojāzāt kardan	مجازات کردن
punishment	mojāzāt	مجازات

fine (penalty)	jarime	جریمه
life imprisonment	habs-e abad	حبس ابد
death penalty	e'dām	اعدام
electric chair	sandali-ye barqi	صندلی برقی
gallows	čube-ye dār	چوبه دار

| to execute (vt) | e'dām kardan | اعدام کردن |
| execution | e'dām | اعدام |

| prison, jail | zendān | زندان |
| cell | sellul-e zendān | سلول زندان |

escort	eskort	اسکورت
prison guard	negahbān zendān	نگهبان زندان
prisoner	zendāni	زندانی

| handcuffs | dastband | دستبند |
| to handcuff (vt) | dastband zadan | دستبند زدن |

prison break	farār	فرار
to break out (vi)	farār kardan	فرار کردن
to disappear (vi)	nāpadid šodan	ناپدید شدن
to release (from prison)	āzād kardan	آزاد کردن
amnesty	afv-e omumi	عفو عمومی

| police | polis | پلیس |
| police officer | polis | پلیس |

police station	kalāntari	كلانترى
billy club	bātum	باتوم
bullhorn	bolandgu	بلندگو
patrol car	māšin-e gašt	ماشين گشت
siren	āžir-e xatar	آژير خطر
to turn on the siren	āžir rā rowšan kardan	آژيررا روشن كردن
siren call	sedā-ye āžir	صداى آژير
crime scene	mahall-e jenāyat	محل جنايت
witness	šāhed	شاهد
freedom	āzādi	آزادى
accomplice	hamdast	همدست
to flee (vi)	maxfi šodan	مخفى شدن
trace (to leave a ~)	rad	رد

163. Police. Law. Part 2

search (investigation)	jostoju	جستجو
to look for ...	jostoju kardan	جستجو كردن
suspicion	šok	شك
suspicious (e.g., ~ vehicle)	maškuk	مشكوك
to stop (cause to halt)	motevaghef kardan	متوقف كردن
to detain (keep in custody)	dastgir kardan	دستگير كردن
case (lawsuit)	parvande	پرونده
investigation	tahqiq	تحقيق
detective	kārāgāh	كارآگاه
investigator	bāzpors	بازپرس
hypothesis	farziye	فرضيه
motive	angize	انگيزه
interrogation	bāzporsi	بازپرسى
to interrogate (vt)	bāzporsi kardan	بازپرسى كردن
to question (~ neighbors, etc.)	estentāq kardan	استنطاق كردن
check (identity ~)	taftiš	تفتيش
round-up	mohāsere	محاصره
search (~ warrant)	taftiš	تفتيش
chase (pursuit)	ta'qib	تعقيب
to pursue, to chase	ta'qib kardan	تعقيب كردن
to track (a criminal)	donbāl kardan	دنبال كردن
arrest	bāzdāšt	بازداشت
to arrest (sb)	bāzdāšt kardan	بازداشت كردن
to catch (thief, etc.)	dastgir kardan	دستگير كردن
capture	dastgiri	دستگيرى
document	sanad	سند
proof (evidence)	esbāt	اثبات

to prove (vt)	esbāt kardan	اثبات کردن
footprint	rad-e pā	رد پا
fingerprints	asar-e angošt	اثر انگشت
piece of evidence	šavāhed	شواهد

alibi	ozr-e qeybat	عذر غیبت
innocent (not guilty)	bi gonāh	بی گناه
injustice	bi edālati	بی عدالتی
unjust, unfair (adj)	ɣeyr-e ādelāne	غیر عادلانه

criminal (adj)	jenāyi	جنایی
to confiscate (vt)	mosādere kardan	مصادره کردن
drug (illegal substance)	mavādd-e moxadder	مواد مخدر
weapon, gun	selāh	سلاح
to disarm (vt)	xæl-e selāh kardan	خلع سلاح کردن
to order (command)	farmān dādan	فرمان دادن
to disappear (vi)	nāpadid šodan	ناپدید شدن

law	qānun	قانون
legal, lawful (adj)	qānuni	قانونی
illegal, illicit (adj)	ɣeyr-e qānuni	غیر قانونی

| responsibility (blame) | mas'uliyat | مسئولیت |
| responsible (adj) | mas'ul | مسئول |

NATURE

The Earth. Part 1

164. Outer space

space	fazā	فضا
space (as adj)	fazāyi	فضایی
outer space	fazā-ye keyhān	فضای کیهان
world	jahān	جهان
universe	giti	گیتی
galaxy	kahkešān	کهکشان
star	setāre	ستاره
constellation	surat-e falaki	صورت فلکی
planet	sayyāre	سیاره
satellite	māhvāre	ماهواره
meteorite	sang-e āsmāni	سنگ آسمانی
comet	setāre-ye donbāle dār	ستارهٔ دنباله دار
asteroid	šahāb	شهاب
orbit	madār	مدار
to revolve (~ around the Earth)	gardidan	گردیدن
atmosphere	jav	جو
the Sun	āftāb	آفتاب
solar system	manzume-ye šamsi	منظومه شمسی
solar eclipse	kosuf	کسوف
the Earth	zamin	زمین
the Moon	māh	ماه
Mars	merrix	مریخ
Venus	zahre	زهره
Jupiter	moštari	مشتری
Saturn	zohal	زحل
Mercury	atārod	عطارد
Uranus	orānus	اورانوس
Neptune	nepton	نپتون
Pluto	poloton	پلوتون
Milky Way	kahkešān rāh-e širi	کهکشان راه شیری

Great Bear (Ursa Major)	dobb-e akbar	دب اکبر
North Star	setāre-ye qotbi	ستاره قطبی
Martian	merrixi	مریخی
extraterrestrial (n)	farā zamini	فرا زمینی
alien	mowjud fazāyi	موجود فضایی
flying saucer	bošqāb-e parande	بشقاب پرنده
spaceship	fazā peymā	فضا پیما
space station	istgāh-e fazāyi	ایستگاه فضایی
blast-off	rāh andāzi	راه اندازی
engine	motor	موتور
nozzle	nāzel	نازل
fuel	suxt	سوخت
cockpit, flight deck	kābin	کابین
antenna	ānten	آنتن
porthole	panjere	پنجره
solar panel	bātri-ye xoršidi	باطری خورشیدی
spacesuit	lebās-e fazānavardi	لباس فضانوردی
weightlessness	bi vazni	بی وزنی
oxygen	oksižen	اکسیژن
docking (in space)	vasl	وصل
to dock (vi, vt)	vasl kardan	وصل کردن
observatory	rasadxāne	رصدخانه
telescope	teleskop	تلسکوپ
to observe (vt)	mošāhede kardan	مشاهده کردن
to explore (vt)	kašf kardan	کشف کردن

165. The Earth

the Earth	zamin	زمین
the globe (the Earth)	kare-ye zamin	کرهٔ زمین
planet	sayyāre	سیاره
atmosphere	jav	جو
geography	joqrāfiyā	جغرافیا
nature	tabi'at	طبیعت
globe (table ~)	kare-ye joqrāfiyāyi	کرهٔ جغرافیایی
map	naqše	نقشه
atlas	atlas	اطلس
Europe	orupā	اروپا
Asia	āsiyā	آسیا
Africa	āfriqā	آفریقا

Australia	ostorāliyā	استرالیا
America	emrikā	امریکا
North America	emrikā-ye šomāli	امریکای شمالی
South America	emrikā-ye jonubi	امریکای جنوبی

| Antarctica | qotb-e jonub | قطب جنوب |
| the Arctic | qotb-e šomāl | قطب شمال |

166. Cardinal directions

north	šomāl	شمال
to the north	be šomāl	به شمال
in the north	dar šomāl	در شمال
northern (adj)	šomāli	شمالی

south	jonub	جنوب
to the south	be jonub	به جنوب
in the south	dar jonub	در جنوب
southern (adj)	jonubi	جنوبی

west	qarb	غرب
to the west	be qarb	به غرب
in the west	dar qarb	در غرب
western (adj)	qarbi	غربی

east	šarq	شرق
to the east	be šarq	به شرق
in the east	dar šarq	در شرق
eastern (adj)	šarqi	شرقی

167. Sea. Ocean

sea	daryā	دریا
ocean	oqyānus	اقیانوس
gulf (bay)	xalij	خلیج
straits	tange	تنگه

| land (solid ground) | zamin | زمین |
| continent (mainland) | qāre | قاره |

island	jazire	جزیره
peninsula	šeb-e jazire	شبه جزیره
archipelago	majma'-ol-jazāyer	مجمع‌الجزایر

bay, cove	xalij-e kučak	خلیج کوچک
harbor	langargāh	لنگرگاه
lagoon	mordāb	مرداب
cape	damāqe	دماغه

atoll	jazire-ye marjāni	جزیره مرجانی
reef	tappe-ye daryāyi	تپه دریایی
coral	marjān	مرجان
coral reef	tappe-ye marjāni	تپه مرجانی
deep (adj)	amiq	عمیق
depth (deep water)	omq	عمق
abyss	partgāh	پرتگاه
trench (e.g., Mariana ~)	derāz godāl	درازگودال
current (Ocean ~)	jaryān	جریان
to surround (bathe)	ehāte kardan	احاطه کردن
shore	sāhel	ساحل
coast	sāhel	ساحل
flow (flood tide)	mod	مد
ebb (ebb tide)	jazr	جزر
shoal	sāhel-e šeni	ساحل شنی
bottom (~ of the sea)	qa'r	قعر
wave	mowj	موج
crest (~ of a wave)	nok	نوک
spume (sea foam)	kaf	کف
storm (sea storm)	tufān-e daryāyi	طوفان دریایی
hurricane	tufān	طوفان
tsunami	sonāmi	سونامی
calm (dead ~)	sokun-e daryā	سکون دریا
quiet, calm (adj)	ārām	آرام
pole	qotb	قطب
polar (adj)	qotbi	قطبی
latitude	arz-e joqrāfiyāyi	عرض جغرافیایی
longitude	tul-e joqrāfiyāyi	طول جغرافیایی
parallel	movāzi	موازی
equator	xatt-e ostavā	خط استوا
sky	āsemān	آسمان
horizon	ofoq	افق
air	havā	هوا
lighthouse	fānus-e daryāyi	فانوس دریایی
to dive (vi)	širje raftan	شیرجه رفتن
to sink (ab. boat)	qarq šodan	غرق شدن
treasures	ganj	گنج

168. Mountains

mountain	kuh	کوه
mountain range	rešte-ye kuh	رشته کوه

mountain ridge	selsele-ye jebāl	سلسله جبال
summit, top	qolle	قله
peak	qolle	قله
foot (~ of the mountain)	dāmane-ye kuh	دامنهٔ کوه
slope (mountainside)	šib	شیب

volcano	ātaš-fešān	آتشفشان
active volcano	ātaš-fešān-e fa'āl	آتش فشان فعال
dormant volcano	ātaš-fešān-e xāmuš	آتش فشان خاموش

eruption	favarān	فوران
crater	dahāne-ye ātašfešān	دهانهٔ آتش فشان
magma	māgmā	ماگما
lava	godāze	گدازه
molten (~ lava)	godāxte	گداخته

canyon	tange	تنگه
gorge	darre-ye tang	دره تنگ
crevice	tange	تنگه
abyss (chasm)	partgāh	پرتگاه

pass, col	gozargāh	گذرگاه
plateau	falāt	فلات
cliff	saxre	صخره
hill	tappe	تپه

glacier	yaxčāl	یخچال
waterfall	ābšār	آبشار
geyser	češme-ye āb-e garm	چشمهٔ آب گرم
lake	daryāče	دریاچه

plain	jolge	جلگه
landscape	manzare	منظره
echo	en'ekās-e sowt	انعکاس صوت

alpinist	kuhnavard	کوهنورد
rock climber	saxre-ye navard	صخره نورد
to conquer (in climbing)	fath kardan	فتح کردن
climb (an easy ~)	so'ud	صعود

169. Rivers

river	rudxāne	رودخانه
spring (natural source)	češme	چشمه
riverbed (river channel)	bastar	بستر
basin (river valley)	howze	حوضه
to flow into ...	rixtan	ریختن

| tributary | enše'āb | انشعاب |
| bank (of river) | sāhel | ساحل |

current (stream)	jaryān	جریان
downstream (adv)	be samt-e pāin-e rudxāne	به سمت پائین رودخانه
upstream (adv)	be samt-e bālā-ye rudxāne	به سمت بالای رودخانه
inundation	seyl	سیل
flooding	toqyān	طغیان
to overflow (vi)	toqyān kardan	طغیان کردن
to flood (vt)	toqyān kardan	طغیان کردن
shallow (shoal)	tangāb	تنگاب
rapids	tondāb	تندآب
dam	sad	سد
canal	kānāl	کانال
reservoir (artificial lake)	maxzan-e āb	مخزن آب
sluice, lock	ābgir	آبگیر
water body (pond, etc.)	maxzan-e āb	مخزن آب
swamp (marshland)	bātlāq	باتلاق
bog, marsh	lajan zār	لجن زار
whirlpool	gerdāb	گرداب
stream (brook)	ravad	رود
drinking (ab. water)	āšāmidani	آشامیدنی
fresh (~ water)	širin	شیرین
ice	yax	یخ
to freeze over (ab. river, etc.)	yax bastan	یخ بستن

170. Forest

forest, wood	jangal	جنگل
forest (as adj)	jangali	جنگلی
thick forest	jangal-e anbuh	جنگل انبوه
grove	biše	بیشه
forest clearing	marqzār	مرغزار
thicket	biše-hā	بیشه ها
scrubland	bute zār	بوته زار
footpath (troddenpath)	kure-ye rāh	کوره راه
gully	darre	دره
tree	deraxt	درخت
leaf	barg	برگ
leaves (foliage)	šāx-o barg	شاخ و برگ
fall of leaves	barg rizi	برگ ریزی
to fall (ab. leaves)	rixtan	ریختن

top (of the tree)	nok	نوک
branch	šāxe	شاخه
bough	šāxe	شاخه
bud (on shrub, tree)	šokufe	شکوفه
needle (of pine tree)	suzan	سوزن
pine cone	maxrut-e kāj	مخروط کاج
hollow (in a tree)	surāx	سوراخ
nest	lāne	لانه
burrow (animal hole)	lāne	لانه
trunk	tane	تنه
root	riše	ریشه
bark	pust	پوست
moss	xaze	خزه
to uproot (remove trees or tree stumps)	rišekan kardan	ریشه کن کردن
to chop down	boridan	بریدن
to deforest (vt)	boridan	بریدن
tree stump	kande-ye deraxt	کندۀ درخت
campfire	ātaš	آتش
forest fire	ātaš suzi	آتش سوزی
to extinguish (vt)	xāmuš kardan	خاموش کردن
forest ranger	jangal bān	جنگل بان
protection	mohāfezat	محافظت
to protect (~ nature)	mohāfezat kardan	محافظت کردن
poacher	šekārči-ye qeyr-e qānuni	شکارچی غیر قانونی
steel trap	tale	تله
to gather, to pick (vt)	čidan	چیدن
to lose one's way	gom šodan	گم شدن

171. Natural resources

natural resources	manābe-'e tabii	منابع طبیعی
minerals	mavādd-e ma'dani	مواد معدنی
deposits	tah nešast	ته نشست
field (e.g., oilfield)	meydān	میدان
to mine (extract)	estexrāj kardan	استخراج کردن
mining (extraction)	estexrāj	استخراج
ore	sang-e ma'dani	سنگ معدنی
mine (e.g., for coal)	ma'dan	معدن
shaft (mine ~)	ma'dan	معدن
miner	ma'dānči	معدنچی
gas (natural ~)	gāz	گاز
gas pipeline	lule-ye gāz	لولۀ گاز

oil (petroleum)	naft	نفت
oil pipeline	lule-ye naft	لولۀ نفت
oil well	čāh-e naft	چاه نفت
derrick (tower)	dakal-e haffāri	دکل حفاری
tanker	tānker	تانکر
sand	šen	شن
limestone	sang-e āhak	سنگ آهک
gravel	sangrize	سنگریزه
peat	turb	تورب
clay	xāk-e ros	خاک رس
coal	zoqāl sang	زغال سنگ
iron (ore)	āhan	آهن
gold	talā	طلا
silver	noqre	نقره
nickel	nikel	نیکل
copper	mes	مس
zinc	ruy	روی
manganese	mangenez	منگنز
mercury	jive	جیوه
lead	sorb	سرب
mineral	mādde-ye ma'dani	مادۀ معدنی
crystal	bolur	بلور
marble	marmar	مرمر
uranium	orāniyom	اورانیوم

The Earth. Part 2

172. Weather

weather	havā	هوا
weather forecast	piš bini havā	پیش بینی هوا
temperature	damā	دما
thermometer	damāsanj	دماسنج
barometer	havāsanj	هواسنج
humid (adj)	martub	مرطوب
humidity	rotubat	رطوبت
heat (extreme ~)	garmā	گرما
hot (torrid)	dāq	داغ
it's hot	havā xeyli garm ast	هوا خیلی گرم است
it's warm	havā garm ast	هوا گرم است
warm (moderately hot)	garm	گرم
it's cold	sard ast	سرد است
cold (adj)	sard	سرد
sun	āftāb	آفتاب
to shine (vi)	tābidan	تابیدن
sunny (day)	āftābi	آفتابی
to come up (vi)	tolu' kardan	طلوع کردن
to set (vi)	qorob kardan	غروب کردن
cloud	abr	ابر
cloudy (adj)	abri	ابری
rain cloud	abr-e bārānzā	ابر باران زا
somber (gloomy)	tire	تیره
rain	bārān	باران
it's raining	bārān mibārad	باران می بارد
rainy (~ day, weather)	bārāni	بارانی
to drizzle (vi)	nam-nam bāridan	نم نم باریدن
pouring rain	bārān šodid	باران شدید
downpour	ragbār	رگبار
heavy (e.g., ~ rain)	šadid	شدید
puddle	čāle	چاله
to get wet (in rain)	xis šodan	خیس شدن
fog (mist)	meh	مه
foggy	meh ālud	مه آلود

| snow | barf | برف |
| it's snowing | barf mibārad | برف می بارد |

173. Severe weather. Natural disasters

thunderstorm	tufān	طوفان
lightning (~ strike)	barq	برق
to flash (vi)	barq zadan	برق زدن

thunder	ra'd	رعد
to thunder (vi)	qorridan	غریدن
it's thundering	ra'd mizanad	رعد می زند

| hail | tagarg | تگرگ |
| it's hailing | tagarg mibārad | تگرگ می بارد |

| to flood (vt) | toqyān kardan | طغیان کردن |
| flood, inundation | seyl | سیل |

earthquake	zamin-larze	زمین لرزه
tremor, quake	tekān	تکان
epicenter	kānun-e zaminlarze	کانون زمین لرزه

| eruption | favarān | فوران |
| lava | godāze | گدازه |

| twister, tornado | gerdbād | گردباد |
| typhoon | tufān | طوفان |

hurricane	tufān	طوفان
storm	tufān	طوفان
tsunami	sonāmi	سونامی

cyclone	gerdbād	گردباد
bad weather	havā-ye bad	هوای بد
fire (accident)	ātaš suzi	آتش سوزی
disaster	balā-ye tabi'i	بلای طبیعی
meteorite	sang-e āsmāni	سنگ آسمانی

avalanche	bahman	بهمن
snowslide	bahman	بهمن
blizzard	kulāk	کولاک
snowstorm	barf-o burān	برف و بوران

Fauna

174. Mammals. Predators

predator	heyvān-e darande	حیوان درنده
tiger	bebar	ببر
lion	šir	شیر
wolf	gorg	گرگ
fox	rubāh	روباه
jaguar	jagvār	جگوار
leopard	palang	پلنگ
cheetah	yuzpalang	یوزپلنگ
black panther	palang-e siyāh	پلنگ سیاه
puma	yuzpalang	یوزپلنگ
snow leopard	palang-e barfi	پلنگ برفی
lynx	siyāh guš	سیاه گوش
coyote	gorg-e sahrāyi	گرگ صحرایی
jackal	šoqāl	شغال
hyena	kaftār	کفتار

175. Wild animals

animal	heyvān	حیوان
beast (animal)	heyvān	حیوان
squirrel	sanjāb	سنجاب
hedgehog	xārpošt	خارپشت
hare	xarguš	خرگوش
rabbit	xarguš	خرگوش
badger	gurkan	گورکن
raccoon	rākon	راکن
hamster	muš-e bozorg	موش بزرگ
marmot	muš-e xormā-ye kuhi	موش خرمای کوهی
mole	muš-e kur	موش کور
mouse	muš	موش
rat	muš-e sahrāyi	موش صحرایی
bat	xoffāš	خفاش
ermine	qāqom	قاقم
sable	samur	سمور

marten	samur	سمور
weasel	rāsu	راسو
mink	tire-ye rāsu	تیره راسو
beaver	sag-e ābi	سگ آبی
otter	samur ābi	سمور آبی
horse	asb	اسب
moose	gavazn	گوزن
deer	āhu	آهو
camel	šotor	شتر
bison	gāvmiš	گاومیش
aurochs	gāv miš	گاو میش
buffalo	bufālo	بوفالو
zebra	gurexar	گورخر
antelope	boz-e kuhi	بز کوهی
roe deer	šukā	شوکا
fallow deer	qazāl	غزال
chamois	boz-e kuhi	بز کوهی
wild boar	gorāz	گراز
whale	nahang	نهنگ
seal	fak	فک
walrus	širmāhi	شیرماهی
fur seal	gorbe-ye ābi	گربۀ آبی
dolphin	delfin	دلفین
bear	xers	خرس
polar bear	xers-e sefid	خرس سفید
panda	pāndā	پاندا
monkey	meymun	میمون
chimpanzee	šampānze	شمپانزه
orangutan	orāngutān	اورانگوتان
gorilla	guril	گوریل
macaque	mākāk	ماکاک
gibbon	gibon	گیبون
elephant	fil	فیل
rhinoceros	kargadan	کرگدن
giraffe	zarrāfe	زرافه
hippopotamus	asb-e ābi	اسب آبی
kangaroo	kāngoro	کانگورو
koala (bear)	kovālā	کوالا
mongoose	xadang	خدنگ
chinchilla	čin čila	چین چیلا
skunk	rāsu-ye badbu	راسوی بدبو
porcupine	taši	تشی

176. Domestic animals

cat	gorbe	گربه
tomcat	gorbe-ye nar	گربهٔ نر
dog	sag	سگ

horse	asb	اسب
stallion (male horse)	asb-e nar	اسب نر
mare	mādiyān	مادیان

cow	gāv	گاو
bull	gāv-e nar	گاو نر
ox	gāv-e axte	گاو اخته

sheep (ewe)	gusfand	گوسفند
ram	gusfand-e nar	گوسفند نر
goat	boz-e mādde	بز ماده
billy goat, he-goat	boz-e nar	بز نر

| donkey | xar | خر |
| mule | qāter | قاطر |

pig, hog	xuk	خوک
piglet	bače-ye xuk	بچهٔ خوک
rabbit	xarguš	خرگوش

| hen (chicken) | morq | مرغ |
| rooster | xorus | خروس |

duck	ordak	اردک
drake	ordak-e nar	اردک نر
goose	qāz	غاز

| tom turkey, gobbler | buqalamun-e nar | بوقلمون نر |
| turkey (hen) | buqalamun-e māde | بوقلمون ماده |

domestic animals	heyvānāt-e ahli	حیوانات اهلی
tame (e.g., ~ hamster)	ahli	اهلی
to tame (vt)	rām kardan	رام کردن
to breed (vt)	parvareš dādan	پرورش دادن

farm	mazrae	مزرعه
poultry	morq-e xānegi	مرغ خانگی
cattle	dām	دام
herd (cattle)	galle	گله

stable	establ	اصطبل
pigpen	āqol xuk	آغل خوک
cowshed	āqol gāv	آغل گاو
rabbit hutch	lanye xarguš	لانه خرگوش
hen house	morq dāni	مرغ دانی

177. Dogs. Dog breeds

dog	sag	سگ
sheepdog	sag-e gele	سگ گله
German shepherd	saɡ-e ĵerman šeperd	سگ ژرمن شپرد
poodle	pudel	پودل
dachshund	sag-e pākutāh	سگ پاکوتاه
bulldog	buldāg	بولداگ
boxer	boksor	بوکسور
mastiff	māstif	ماستیف
Rottweiler	rotveylir	روتویلر
Doberman	dobermen	دوبرمن
basset	ba's-at	باسیت
bobtail	dam čatri	دم چتری
Dalmatian	dālmāsi	دالماسی
cocker spaniel	kākir spāniyel	کاکیر سپانیبل
Newfoundland	nyufāundland	نیوفاوندلند
Saint Bernard	sant bernārd	سنت برنارد
husky	sag-e surtme	سگ سورتمه
Chow Chow	čāu-čāu	چاو-چاو
spitz	espitz	اسپیتز
pug	pāg	پاگ

178. Sounds made by animals

barking (n)	vāq vāq	واق واق
to bark (vi)	vāq-vāq kardan	واق واق کردن
to meow (vi)	miyu-miyu kardan	میو میو کردن
to purr (vi)	xor-xor kardan	خرخر کردن
to moo (vi)	mu-mu kardan	مو مو کردن
to bellow (bull)	na're kešidan	نعره کشیدن
to growl (vi)	qorqor kardan	غرغر کردن
howl (n)	zuze	زوزه
to howl (vi)	zuze kešidan	زوزه کشیدن
to whine (vi)	zuze kešidan	زوزه کشیدن
to bleat (sheep)	ba'ba' kardan	بع بع کردن
to oink, to grunt (pig)	xor-xor kardan	خرخر کردن
to squeal (vi)	jiq zadan	جیغ زدن
to croak (vi)	qur-qur kardan	قورقور کردن
to buzz (insect)	vez-vez kardan	وزوز کردن
to chirp (crickets, grasshopper)	jir-jir kardan	جیر جیر کردن

179. Birds

bird	parande	پرنده
pigeon	kabutar	کبوتر
sparrow	gonješk	گنجشک
tit (great tit)	morq-e zanburxār	مرغ زنبورخوار
magpie	zāqi	زاغی
raven	kalāq-e siyāh	کلاغ سیاه
crow	kalāq	کلاغ
jackdaw	zāq	زاغ
rook	kalāq-e siyāh	کلاغ سیاه
duck	ordak	اردک
goose	qāz	غاز
pheasant	qarqāvol	قرقاول
eagle	oqāb	عقاب
hawk	qerqi	قرقی
falcon	šāhin	شاهین
vulture	karkas	کرکس
condor (Andean ~)	karkas-e emrikāyi	کرکس امریکایی
swan	qu	قو
crane	dornā	درنا
stork	lak lak	لک لک
parrot	tuti	طوطی
hummingbird	morq-e magas-e xār	مرغ مگس خوار
peacock	tāvus	طاووس
ostrich	šotormorq	شترمرغ
heron	havāsil	حواصیل
flamingo	felāmingo	فلامینگو
pelican	pelikān	پلیکان
nightingale	bolbol	بلبل
swallow	parastu	پرستو
thrush	bāstarak	باسترک
song thrush	torqe	طرقه
blackbird	tukā-ye siyāh	توکای سیاه
swift	bādxorak	بادخورک
lark	čakāvak	چکاوک
quail	belderčin	بلدرچین
woodpecker	dārkub	دارکوب
cuckoo	fāxte	فاخته
owl	joqd	جغد
eagle owl	šāh buf	شاه بوف

wood grouse	siāh xorus	سیاه خروس
black grouse	siāh xorus-e jangali	سیاه خروس جنگلی
partridge	kabk	کبک

starling	sār	سار
canary	qanāri	قناری
hazel grouse	siyāh xorus-e fandoqi	سیاه خروس فندقی
chaffinch	sehre-ye jangali	سهره جنگلی
bullfinch	sohre sar-e siyāh	سهره سر سیاه

seagull	morq-e daryāyi	مرغ دریایی
albatross	morq-e daryāyi	مرغ دریایی
penguin	pangoan	پنگوئن

180. Birds. Singing and sounds

to sing (vi)	xāndan	خواندن
to call (animal, bird)	faryād kardan	فریاد کردن
to crow (rooster)	ququli ququ kardan	قوقولی قوقو کردن
cock-a-doodle-doo	ququli ququ	قوقولی قوقو

to cluck (hen)	qodqod kardan	قدقد کردن
to caw (vi)	qār-qār kardan	قارقار کردن
to quack (duck)	qāt-qāt kardan	قات قات کردن
to cheep (vi)	jir-jir kardan	جیر جیر کردن
to chirp, to twitter	jik-jik kardan	جیک جیک کردن

181. Fish. Marine animals

bream	māhi-ye sim	ماهی سیم
carp	kapur	کپور
perch	māhi-e luti	ماهی لوتی
catfish	gorbe-ye māhi	گربه ماهی
pike	ordak māhi	اردک ماهی

| salmon | māhi-ye salemon | ماهی سالمون |
| sturgeon | māhi-ye xāviār | ماهی خاویار |

herring	māhi-ye šur	ماهی شور
Atlantic salmon	sālmon-e atlāntik	سالمون اتلانتیک
mackerel	māhi-ye esqumeri	ماهی اسقومری
flatfish	sofre māhi	سفره ماهی

zander, pike perch	suf	سوف
cod	māhi-ye rowqan	ماهی روغن
tuna	tan māhi	تن ماهی
trout	māhi-ye qezelālā	ماهی قزل آلا
eel	mārmāhi	مارماهی

electric ray	partomahiye barqi	پرتوماهی برقی
moray eel	mārmāhi	مارماهی
piranha	pirānā	پیرانا
shark	kuse-ye māhi	کوسه ماهی
dolphin	delfin	دلفین
whale	nahang	نهنگ
crab	xarčang	خرچنگ
jellyfish	arus-e daryāyi	عروس دریایی
octopus	hašt pā	هشت پا
starfish	setāre-ye daryāyi	ستاره دریایی
sea urchin	xārpošt-e daryāyi	خارپشت دریایی
seahorse	asb-e daryāyi	اسب دریایی
oyster	sadaf-e xorāki	صدف خوراکی
shrimp	meygu	میگو
lobster	xarčang-e daryāyi	خرچنگ دریایی
spiny lobster	xarčang-e xārdār	خرچنگ خاردار

182. Amphibians. Reptiles

snake	mār	مار
venomous (snake)	sammi	سمی
viper	af'i	افعی
cobra	kobrā	کبرا
python	mār-e pinton	مار پیتون
boa	mār-e bwa	مار بوا
grass snake	mār-e čaman	مار چمن
rattle snake	mār-e zangi	مار زنگی
anaconda	mār-e ānākondā	مار آناکوندا
lizard	susmār	سوسمار
iguana	susmār-e deraxti	سوسمار درختی
monitor lizard	bozmajje	بزمجه
salamander	samandar	سمندر
chameleon	āftāb-parast	آفتاب پرست
scorpion	aqrab	عقرب
turtle	lāk pošt	لاک پشت
frog	qurbāqe	قورباغه
toad	vazaq	وزغ
crocodile	temsāh	تمساح

183. Insects

insect, bug	hašare	حشره
butterfly	parvāne	پروانه
ant	murče	مورچه
fly	magas	مگس
mosquito	paše	پشه
beetle	susk	سوسک

wasp	zanbur	زنبور
bee	zanbur-e asal	زنبور عسل
bumblebee	xar zanbur	خرزنبور
gadfly (botfly)	xarmagas	خرمگس

| spider | ankabut | عنکبوت |
| spiderweb | tār-e ankabut | تارعنکبوت |

dragonfly	sanjāqak	سنجاقک
grasshopper	malax	ملخ
moth (night butterfly)	bid	بید

cockroach	susk	سوسک
tick	kane	کنه
flea	kak	کک
midge	paše-ye rize	پشه ریزه

locust	malax	ملخ
snail	halazun	حلزون
cricket	jirjirak	جیرجیرک
lightning bug	kerm-e šab-tāb	کرم شب تاب
ladybug	kafšduzak	کفشدوزک
cockchafer	susk bāldār	سوسک بالدار

leech	zālu	زالو
caterpillar	kerm-e abrišam	کرم ابریشم
earthworm	kerm	کرم
larva	lārv	لارو

184. Animals. Body parts

beak	nok	نوک
wings	bāl-hā	بال ها
foot (of bird)	panje	پنجه
feathers (plumage)	por-o bāl	پر و بال
feather	por	پر
crest	kākol	کاکل

| gills | ābšoš | آبشش |
| spawn | toxme mahi | تخم ماهی |

187

larva	lārv	لارو
fin	bāle-ye māhi	باله ماهی
scales (of fish, reptile)	fals	فلس

fang (canine)	niš	نیش
paw (e.g., cat's ~)	panje	پنجه
muzzle (snout)	puze	پوزه
mouth (of cat, dog)	dahān	دهان
tail	dam	دم
whiskers	sebil	سبیل

| hoof | sam | سم |
| horn | šāx | شاخ |

carapace	lāk	لاک
shell (of mollusk)	sadaf	صدف
eggshell	puste	پوسته

| animal's hair (pelage) | pašm | پشم |
| pelt (hide) | pust | پوست |

185. Animals. Habitats

| habitat | zistgāh | زیستگاه |
| migration | mohājerat | مهاجرت |

mountain	kuh	کوه
reef	tappe-ye daryāyi	تپه دریایی
cliff	saxre	صخره

forest	jangal	جنگل
jungle	jangal	جنگل
savanna	sāvānā	ساوانا
tundra	tondrā	توندرا

steppe	estep	استپ
desert	biyābān	بیابان
oasis	vāhe	واحه

sea	daryā	دریا
lake	daryāče	دریاچه
ocean	oqyānus	اقیانوس

swamp (marshland)	bātlāq	باتلاق
freshwater (adj)	ab-e širin	آب شیرین
pond	tālāb	تالاب
river	rudxāne	رودخانه

| den (bear's ~) | lāne-ye xers | لانه خرس |
| nest | lāne | لانه |

hollow (in a tree)	surāx	سوراخ
burrow (animal hole)	lāne	لانه
anthill	lāne-ye murče	لانۀ مورچه

Flora

186. Trees

tree	deraxt	درخت
deciduous (adj)	barg riz	برگ ریز
coniferous (adj)	maxrutiyān	مخروطیان
evergreen (adj)	hamiše sabz	همیشه سبز

apple tree	deraxt-e sib	درخت سیب
pear tree	golābi	گلابی
sweet cherry tree	gilās	گیلاس
sour cherry tree	ālbālu	آلبالو
plum tree	ālu	آلو

birch	tus	توس
oak	balut	بلوط
linden tree	zirfun	زیرفون
aspen	senowbar-e larzān	صنوبر لرزان
maple	afrā	افرا

spruce	senowbar	صنوبر
pine	kāj	کاج
larch	senowbar-e ārāste	صنوبر آراسته
fir tree	šāh deraxt	شاه درخت
cedar	sedr	سدر

poplar	sepidār	سپیدار
rowan	zabān gonješk-e kuhi	زبان گنجشک کوهی
willow	bid	بید
alder	tuskā	توسکا

beech	rāš	راش
elm	nārvan-e qermez	نارون قرمز

ash (tree)	zabān-e gonješk	زبان گنجشک
chestnut	šāh balut	شاه بلوط

magnolia	māgnoliyā	ماگنولیا
palm tree	naxl	نخل
cypress	sarv	سرو

mangrove	karnā	کرنا
baobab	bāobāb	بائوباب
eucalyptus	okaliptus	اوکالیپتوس
sequoia	sorx-e čub	سرخ چوب

187. Shrubs

bush	bute	بوته
shrub	bute zār	بوته زار
grapevine	angur	انگور
vineyard	tākestān	تاکستان
raspberry bush	tamešk	تمشک
blackcurrant bush	angur-e farangi-ye siyāh	انگور فرنگی سیاه
redcurrant bush	angur-e farangi-ye sorx	انگور فرنگی سرخ
gooseberry bush	angur-e farangi	انگور فرنگی
acacia	aqāqiyā	اقاقیا
barberry	zerešk	زرشک
jasmine	yāsaman	یاسمن
juniper	ardaj	اردج
rosebush	bute-ye gol-e mohammadi	بوتۀ گل محمدی
dog rose	nastaran	نسترن

188. Mushrooms

mushroom	qārč	قارچ
edible mushroom	qārč-e xorāki	قارچ خوراکی
poisonous mushroom	qārč-e sammi	قارچ سمی
cap (of mushroom)	kolāhak-e qārč	کلاهک قارچ
stipe (of mushroom)	pāye	پایه
cep (Boletus edulis)	qārč-e sefid	قارچ سفید
orange-cap boletus	samāruq	سماروق
birch bolete	qārč-e bulet	قارچ بولت
chanterelle	qārč-e zard	قارچ زرد
russula	qārč-e tiqe-ye tord	قارچ تیغه ترد
morel	qārč-e morkelā	قارچ مورکلا
fly agaric	qārč-e magas	قارچ مگس
death cap	kolāhak-e marg	کلاهک مرگ

189. Fruits. Berries

fruit	mive	میوه
fruits	mive jāt	میوه جات
apple	sib	سیب
pear	golābi	گلابی
plum	ālu	آلو

strawberry (garden ~)	tut-e farangi	توت فرنگی
sour cherry	ālbālu	آلبالو
sweet cherry	gilās	گیلاس
grape	angur	انگور
raspberry	tamešk	تمشک
blackcurrant	angur-e farangi-ye siyāh	انگور فرنگی سیاه
redcurrant	angur-e farangi-ye sorx	انگور فرنگی سرخ
gooseberry	angur-e farangi	انگور فرنگی
cranberry	nārdānak-e vahši	ناردانک وحشی
orange	porteqāl	پرتقال
mandarin	nārengi	نارنگی
pineapple	ānānās	آناناس
banana	mowz	موز
date	xormā	خرما
lemon	limu	لیمو
apricot	zardālu	زردآلو
peach	holu	هلو
kiwi	kivi	کیوی
grapefruit	gerip forut	گریپ فوروت
berry	mive-ye butei	میوهٔ بوته ای
berries	mivehā-ye butei	میوه های بوته ای
cowberry	tut-e farangi-ye jangali	توت فرنگی جنگلی
wild strawberry	zoqāl axte	زغال اخته
bilberry	zoqāl axte	زغال اخته

190. Flowers. Plants

flower	gol	گل
bouquet (of flowers)	daste-ye gol	دسته گل
rose (flower)	gol-e sorx	گل سرخ
tulip	lāle	لاله
carnation	mixak	میخک
gladiolus	susan-e sefid	سوسن سفید
cornflower	gol-e gandom	گل گندم
harebell	gol-e estekāni	گل استکانی
dandelion	gol-e qāsedak	گل قاصدک
camomile	bābune	بابونه
aloe	oloviye	آلوئه
cactus	kāktus	کاکتوس
rubber plant, ficus	fikus	فیکوس
lily	susan	سوسن
geranium	gol-e šam'dāni	گل شمعدانی

hyacinth	sonbol	سنبل
mimosa	mimosā	میموسا
narcissus	narges	نرگس
nasturtium	gol-e lādan	گل لادن
orchid	orkide	ارکیده
peony	gol-e ašrafi	گل اشرفی
violet	banafše	بنفشه

pansy	banafše-ye farangi	بنفشه فرنگی
forget-me-not	gol-e farāmuš-am makon	گل فراموشم مکن
daisy	gol-e morvārid	گل مروارید

poppy	xašxāš	خشخاش
hemp	šāh dāne	شاه دانه
mint	naʿnāʿ	نعناع

lily of the valley	muge	موگه
snowdrop	gol-e barfi	گل برفی
nettle	gazane	گزنه
sorrel	toršak	ترشک
water lily	nilufar-e abi	نیلوفر آبی
fern	saraxs	سرخس
lichen	golesang	گلسنگ

greenhouse (tropical ~)	golxāne	گلخانه
lawn	čaman	چمن
flowerbed	baqče-ye gol	باغچه گل

plant	giyāh	گیاه
grass	alaf	علف
blade of grass	alaf	علف

leaf	barg	برگ
petal	golbarg	گلبرگ
stem	sāqe	ساقه
tuber	riše	ریشه

| young plant (shoot) | javāne | جوانه |
| thorn | xār | خار |

to blossom (vi)	gol kardan	گل کردن
to fade, to wither	pažmorde šodan	پژمرده شدن
smell (odor)	bu	بو
to cut (flowers)	boridan	بریدن
to pick (a flower)	kandan	کندن

191. Cereals, grains

| grain | dāne | دانه |
| cereal crops | qallāt | غلات |

ear (of barley, etc.)	xuše	خوشه
wheat	gandom	گندم
rye	čāvdār	چاودار
oats	jow-e sahrāyi	جو صحرایی
millet	arzan	ارزن
barley	jow	جو
corn	zorrat	ذرت
rice	berenj	برنج
buckwheat	gandom-e siyāh	گندم سیاه
pea plant	noxod	نخود
kidney bean	lubiyā qermez	لوبیا قرمز
soy	sowyā	سویا
lentil	adas	عدس
beans (pulse crops)	lubiyā	لوبیا

REGIONAL GEOGRAPHY

Countries. Nationalities

192. Politics. Government. Part 1

politics	siyāsat	سیاست
political (adj)	siyāsi	سیاسی
politician	siyāsatmadār	سیاستمدار
state (country)	dowlat	دولت
citizen	šahrvand	شهروند
citizenship	šahrvandi	شهروندی
national emblem	nešān melli	نشان ملی
national anthem	sorud-e melli	سرود ملی
government	hokumat	حکومت
head of state	rahbar-e dowlat	رهبر دولت
parliament	pārlemān	پارلمان
party	hezb	حزب
capitalism	sarmāye dāri	سرمایه داری
capitalist (adj)	kāpitālisti	کاپیتالیستی
socialism	sosiyālism	سوسیالیسم
socialist (adj)	sosiyālisti	سوسیالیستی
communism	komonism	کمونیسم
communist (adj)	komonisti	کمونیستی
communist (n)	komonist	کمونیست
democracy	demokrāsi	دموکراسی
democrat	demokrāt	دموکرات
democratic (adj)	demokrātik	دموکراتیک
Democratic party	hezb-e demokrāt	حزب دموکرات
liberal (n)	liberāl	لیبرال
liberal (adj)	liberāli	لیبرالی
conservative (n)	mohāfeze kār	محافظه کار
conservative (adj)	mohāfeze kāri	محافظه کاری
republic (n)	jomhuri	جمهوری
republican (n)	jomhuri xāh	جمهوری خواه

Republican party	hezb-e jomhurixāh	حزب جمهوری خواه
elections	entexābāt	انتخابات
to elect (vt)	entexāb kardan	انتخاب کردن
elector, voter	entexāb konande	انتخاب کننده
election campaign	kampeyn-e entexābāti	کمپین انتخاباتی

voting (n)	axz-e ra'y	اخذ رأی
to vote (vi)	ra'y dādan	رأی دادن
suffrage, right to vote	haqq-e ra'y	حق رأی

candidate	nāmzad	نامزد
to be a candidate	nāmzad šodan	نامزد شدن
campaign	kampeyn	کمپین

| opposition (as adj) | moxālef | مخالف |
| opposition (n) | opozisyon | اپوزیسیون |

visit	vizit	ویزیت
official visit	vizit-e rasmi	ویزیت رسمی
international (adj)	beynolmelali	بین المللی

| negotiations | mozākerāt | مذاکرات |
| to negotiate (vi) | mozākere kardan | مذاکره کردن |

193. Politics. Government. Part 2

society	jam'iyat	جمعیت
constitution	qānun-e asāsi	قانون اساسی
power (political control)	hākemiyat	حاکمیت
corruption	fesād	فساد

| law (justice) | qānun | قانون |
| legal (legitimate) | qānuni | قانونی |

| justice (fairness) | edālat | عدالت |
| just (fair) | ādel | عادل |

committee	komite	کمیته
bill (draft law)	lāyehe-ye qānun	لایحهٔ قانون
budget	budje	بودجه
policy	siyāsat	سیاست
reform	eslāhāt	اصلاحات
radical (adj)	efrāti	افراطی

power (strength, force)	niru	نیرو
powerful (adj)	moqtader	مقتدر
supporter	tarafdār	طرفدار
influence	ta'sir	تأثیر
regime (e.g., military ~)	nezām	نظام
conflict	dargiri	درگیری

| conspiracy (plot) | towtee | توطئه |
| provocation | tahrik | تحریک |

to overthrow (regime, etc.)	sarnegun kardan	سرنگون کردن
overthrow (of government)	sarneguni	سرنگونی
revolution	enqelāb	انقلاب

| coup d'état | kudetā | کودتا |
| military coup | kudetā-ye nezāmi | کودتای نظامی |

crisis	bohrān	بحران
economic recession	rokud-e eqtesādi	رکود اقتصادی
demonstrator (protester)	tazāhorāt konande	تظاهرات کننده
demonstration	tazāhorāt	تظاهرات
martial law	hālat-e nezāmi	حالت نظامی
military base	pāygāh-e nezāmi	پایگاه نظامی

| stability | sobāt | ثبات |
| stable (adj) | bāsobāt | باثبات |

| exploitation | bahre bardār-i | بهره برداری |
| to exploit (workers) | bahre bardār-i kardan | بهره برداری کردن |

racism	nežādparasti	نژادپرستی
racist	nežādparast	نژادپرست
fascism	fāšizm	فاشیزم
fascist	fāšist	فاشیست

194. Countries. Miscellaneous

foreigner	xāreji	خارجی
foreign (adj)	xāreji	خارجی
abroad (in a foreign country)	dar xārej	در خارج

emigrant	mohājer	مهاجر
emigration	mohājerat	مهاجرت
to emigrate (vi)	mohājerat kardan	مهاجرت کردن

the West	qarb	غرب
the East	xāvar	خاور
the Far East	xāvar-e-dur	خاوردور

civilization	tamaddon	تمدن
humanity (mankind)	ensāniyat	انسانیت
the world (earth)	jahān	جهان
peace	solh	صلح
worldwide (adj)	jahāni	جهانی
homeland	vatan	وطن
people (population)	mellat	ملت

population	mardom	مردم
people (a lot of ~)	afrād	افراد
nation (people)	mellat	ملت
generation	nasl	نسل
territory (area)	qalamrow	قلمرو
region	mantaqe	منطقه
state (part of a country)	eyālat	ایالت
tradition	sonnat	سنت
custom (tradition)	ādat	عادت
ecology	mohit-e zist	محیط زیست
Indian (Native American)	hendi	هندی
Gypsy (masc.)	mard-e kowli	مرد کولی
Gypsy (fem.)	zan-e kowli	زن کولی
Gypsy (adj)	kowli	کولی
empire	emperāturi	امپراطوری
colony	mosta'mere	مستعمره
slavery	bardegi	بردگی
invasion	tahājom	تهاجم
famine	gorosnegi	گرسنگی

195. Major religious groups. Confessions

religion	din	دین
religious (adj)	dini	دینی
faith, belief	e'teqād	اعتقاد
to believe (in God)	e'teqād dāštan	اعتقاد داشتن
believer	mo'men	مؤمن
atheism	bi dini	بی دینی
atheist	molhed	ملحد
Christianity	masihiyat	مسیحیت
Christian (n)	masihi	مسیحی
Christian (adj)	masihi	مسیحی
Catholicism	mazhab-e kātolik	مذهب کاتولیک
Catholic (n)	kātolik	کاتولیک
Catholic (adj)	kātolik	کاتولیک
Protestantism	āin-e porotestān	آئین پروتستان
Protestant Church	kelisā-ye porotestān	کلیسای پروتستان
Protestant (n)	porotestān	پروتستان
Orthodoxy	mazhab-e ortodoks	مذهب ارتدوکس
Orthodox Church	kelisā-ye ortodoks	کلیسای ارتدوکس

Orthodox (n)	ortodoks	ارتدوکس
Presbyterianism	persbiterinism	پرسبیترینیسم
Presbyterian Church	kelisā-ye persbiteri	کلیسای پرسبیتری
Presbyterian (n)	persbiteri	پرسبیتری

| Lutheranism | kelisā-ye lutrān | کلیسای لوتران |
| Lutheran (n) | lutrān | لوتران |

| Baptist Church | kelisā-ye baptist | کلیسای باپتیست |
| Baptist (n) | baptist | باپتیست |

| Anglican Church | kelisā-ye anglikān | کلیسای انگلیکان |
| Anglican (n) | anglikān | انگلیکان |

| Mormonism | farqe-ye mormon | فرقه مورمون |
| Mormon (n) | mormon | مورمون |

| Judaism | yahudiyat | یهودیت |
| Jew (n) | yahudi | یهودی |

| Buddhism | budism | بودیسم |
| Buddhist (n) | budāyi | بودایی |

| Hinduism | hendi | هندی |
| Hindu (n) | hendu | هندو |

Islam	eslām	اسلام
Muslim (n)	mosalmān	مسلمان
Muslim (adj)	mosalmāni	مسلمانی

| Shiah Islam | ši'e | شیعه |
| Shiite (n) | ši'e | شیعه |

| Sunni Islam | senni | سنی |
| Sunnite (n) | senni | سنی |

196. Religions. Priests

| priest | kešiš | کشیش |
| the Pope | pāp | پاپ |

monk, friar	rāheb	راهب
nun	rāhebe	راهبه
pastor	pišvā-ye ruhān-i	پیشوای روحانی

abbot	rāheb-e bozorg	راهب بزرگ
vicar (parish priest)	keš-yaš baxš	کشیش بخش
bishop	osqof	اسقف
cardinal	kārdināl	کاردینال
preacher	vā'ez	واعظ

| preaching | mo'eze | موعظه |
| parishioners | kešiš tabār | کشیش تبار |

| believer | mo'men | مؤمن |
| atheist | molhed | ملحد |

197. Faith. Christianity. Islam

| Adam | ādam | آدم |
| Eve | havvā | حوا |

God	xodā	خدا
the Lord	xodā	خدا
the Almighty	xodā	خدا

sin	gonāh	گناه
to sin (vi)	gonāh kardan	گناه کردن
sinner (masc.)	gonāhkār	گناهکار
sinner (fem.)	gonāhkār	گناهکار

| hell | jahannam | جهنم |
| paradise | behešt | بهشت |

| Jesus | isā | عیسی |
| Jesus Christ | isā masih | عیسی مسیح |

the Holy Spirit	ruh olqodos	روح القدس
the Savior	monji	منجی
the Virgin Mary	maryam bākere	مریم باکره

the Devil	šeytān	شیطان
devil's (adj)	šeytāni	شیطانی
Satan	šeytān	شیطان
satanic (adj)	šeytāni	شیطانی

angel	ferešte	فرشته
guardian angel	ferešte-ye negahbān	فرشتهٔ نگهبان
angelic (adj)	ferešte i	فرشته ای

apostle	havāri	حواری
archangel	ferešte-ye moqarrab	فرشتهٔ مقرب
the Antichrist	dajjāl	دجال

Church	kelisā	کلیسا
Bible	enjil	انجیل
biblical (adj)	enjili	انجیلی

Old Testament	ahd-e atiq	عهد عتیق
New Testament	ahd-e jadid	عهد جدید
Gospel	enjil	انجیل

Holy Scripture	ketāb-e moqaddas	کتاب مقدس
Heaven	behešt	بهشت
Commandment	farmān	فرمان
prophet	payāmbar	پیامبر
prophecy	payāmbari	پیامبری
Allah	allāh	الله
Mohammed	mohammad	محمد
the Koran	qor'ān	قرآن
mosque	masjed	مسجد
mullah	mala'	ملا
prayer	namāz	نماز
to pray (vi, vt)	do'ā kardan	دعا کردن
pilgrimage	ziyārat	زیارت
pilgrim	zāer	زائر
Mecca	makke	مکه
church	kelisā	کلیسا
temple	haram	حرم
cathedral	kelisā-ye jāme'	کلیسای جامع
Gothic (adj)	gotik	گوتیک
synagogue	kenešt	کنشت
mosque	masjed	مسجد
chapel	kelisā-ye kučak	کلیسای کوچک
abbey	sowme'e	صومعه
convent	sowme'e	صومعه
monastery	deyr	دیر
bell (church ~s)	nāqus	ناقوس
bell tower	borj-e nāqus	برج ناقوس
to ring (ab. bells)	sedā kardan	صدا کردن
cross	salib	صلیب
cupola (roof)	gonbad	گنبد
icon	šamāyel-e moqaddas	شمایل مقدس
soul	jān	جان
fate (destiny)	sarnevešt	سرنوشت
evil (n)	badi	بدی
good (n)	niki	نیکی
vampire	xun āšām	خون آشام
witch (evil ~)	jādugar	جادوگر
demon	div	دیو
spirit	ruh	روح
redemption (giving us ~)	talab-e afv	طلب عفو
to redeem (vt)	talab-e afv kardan	طلب عفو کردن

church service, mass	ebādat	عبادت
to say mass	ebādat kardan	عبادت کردن
confession	marāsem-e towbe	مراسم توبه
to confess (vi)	towbe kardan	توبه کردن
saint (n)	qeddis	قدیس
sacred (holy)	moqaddas	مقدس
holy water	āb-e moqaddas	آب مقدس
ritual (n)	marāsem	مراسم
ritual (adj)	āyini	آیینی
sacrifice	qorbāni	قربانی
superstition	xorāfe	خرافه
superstitious (adj)	xorāfāti	خرافاتی
afterlife	zendegi pas az marg	زندگی پس ازمرگ
eternal life	zendegi-ye jāvid	زندگی جاوید

MISCELLANEOUS

198. Various useful words

background (green ~)	zamine	زمينه
balance (of situation)	ta'ādol	تعادل
barrier (obstacle)	hesār	حصار
base (basis)	pāye	پايه
beginning	šoru'	شروع
category	tabaqe	طبقه
cause (reason)	sabab	سبب
choice	entexāb	انتخاب
coincidence	tatāboq	تطابق
comfortable (~ chair)	rāhat	راحت
comparison	qiyās	قياس
compensation	jobrān	جبران
degree (extent, amount)	daraje	درجه
development	pišraft	پيشرفت
difference	farq	فرق
effect (e.g., of drugs)	asar	اثر
effort (exertion)	kušeš	كوشش
element	onsor	عنصر
end (finish)	etmām	اتمام
example (illustration)	mesāl	مثال
fact	haqiqat	حقيقت
frequent (adj)	mokarrar	مكرر
growth (development)	rošd	رشد
help	komak	كمك
ideal	ide āl	ايده آل
kind (sort, type)	no'	نوع
labyrinth	hezār tuy	هزارتوى
mistake, error	eštebāh	اشتباه
moment	lahze	لحظه
object (thing)	mabhas	مبحث
obstacle	māne'	مانع
original (original copy)	asli	اصلى
part (~ of sth)	joz	جزء
particle, small part	zarre	ذره
pause (break)	maks	مكث

position	vaz'	وضع
principle	asl	اصل
problem	moškel	مشکل
process	ravand	روند
progress	taraqqi	ترقی
property (quality)	xāsiyat	خاصیت
reaction	vākoneš	واکنش
risk	risk	ریسک
secret	rāz	راز
series	seri	سری
shape (outer form)	šekl	شکل
situation	vaz'iyat	وضعیت
solution	hal	حل
standard (adj)	estāndārd	استاندارد
standard (level of quality)	estāndārd	استاندارد
stop (pause)	tavaqqof	توقف
style	sabok	سبک
system	sistem	سیستم
table (chart)	jadval	جدول
tempo, rate	sor'at	سرعت
term (word, expression)	estelāh	اصطلاح
thing (object, item)	čiz	چیز
truth (e.g., moment of ~)	haqiqat	حقیقت
turn (please wait your ~)	nowbat	نوبت
type (sort, kind)	no'	نوع
urgent (adj)	fowri	فوری
urgently (adv)	foran	فوراً
utility (usefulness)	fāyede	فایده
variant (alternative)	moteqayyer	متغیر
way (means, method)	tariq	طریق
zone	mantaqe	منطقه